Forever

in

Bloom

Poetry Collection

AnnaMarie Antoski

ISBN-13: 978-0-9868844-6-7

DEDICATION

To Bubba

CONTENTS

ACKNOWLEDGMENTS

To all who are blossoming through life
consciously and unconditionally

Chapter 1

Stumbling Through Infinity

Stumbling through Infinity
With only glitches that triggered me
Ever since my birth, bits of reflections sparked
At first not much to keep it shining
Because as a baby I came into this world crying

Could it be because I knew amnesia would set in
Filtering my perception from the spiritual realm
Altering me from my original plan
No matter how much I wondered from my spiritual clan
This time my blueprint was to remember to thin the veil

With necessities of relearning how to function in this body
When just before I was so free in divinity
Now constricted to do it all over again
This time to allow the spiritual remembrance to be my guide
Leaving post signs to follow of love,
bliss and serenity to reside

Deep down in my soul
Even when the ego took it's hold
Trying to guide me to do what I was told
My rebellious spiritual nature prodded me to explore
As it always knows the expanding roads that I should soar
As I stumble through Infinity,
to finally find my way once more

Physical Caretakers in our Souls Blueprint

Through such eternal grace I was born to a family of love
Their first baby born, yes me, a newborn baby girl
As I looked upon them to take care of me
Teach me to handle and survive in this world so profound
No matter what conditioning there was being programmed
There was one blueprint that was most important I found
Of unconditional love that would allow me to accept and release
To eventually master no more judgments in all I perceive
And live this live with divine guidance as the key

Could it be that before birth
We have a blueprint to try to follow
Of greater depths that urge from our soul
To do what we didn't do on our last physical journey through birth
We take the leaping plunge
Like a dive in seeming unknown territory
                                    of physical realities abyss
Yet deep down always lingering
Is our memories imprinted in our soul
To remember and do it again
From whispering urgings when we listen we know
Does it resonate with you as it does for me
That we really can be all we have been challenged to be

Through humanity's perpetual past
To final remember and bring it into our powerful now at last
That we can undo lingering tainted memories
As we create our souls exuberance along our way
To never forget again
That we are infinite spiritual beings forever
And these physical bodies are just the Infinite Creators game
That we play in like infinite hide and seek
Sometimes we stumble so far
But our infinite creator always knows
Even when we believe we are so lost
We are always one thought away to being back home

ROADS OF LIFE OPPORTUNITIES

Into physical we travel
With infinite spirit into embodiment
We encounter many sign posts along our way
Though many times our journey's path
Is not paved so gracefully

Yet when we listen to the gentlest whispers
That resonate with our loving hearts
Even the most stormiest roads we may find ourselves on
Will be filled with opportunities
To take all seeming negativity
And transform it into a positive
Returning us to infinite love
Then nothing is ever too great
That we cannot forsake
When we keep listening with our hearts

Blossoming Forever

What else could it be
since we jumped upon this physical experience of reality,
and bravely go to do it all over again, Yikes,
might be our quick reply
when its so much easier to decide
without physical body and reality that can weigh us down
it seems to me so appropriately
to label it,
blossoming forever while physical bound

As I wonder, do we ever really fully bloom?
When continuously we keep learning to know
Hence once we know then another learning curve indeed pops up,
keeping us forever wanting to bloom,
only till the next urging comes forth,
to do it all over again, stretch ourselves even more,
every time we may think we are done,
oops, again, there's something more, let's make it fun

Blossoming forever is what we seem so great at
even though we may have to relearn it over and over
Extend, expand, stretch ourselves to explore
to keep blossoming eternally,
ah when will we know we are finally done,
possibly when all desires urge us no longer to want
and we are just joyfully content and free

Sleep Blossoms
into
Desires Manifested

As I lie myself down to sleep
So many thoughts swirl around my mind to seek
Old habits that in the past were worrisome
Have now become of desires that will bloom
All the old thoughts become forgotten memories
While my desires will be manifested soon

Knowing these thoughts are the tiny seeds
That my brain and body constantly receive
Taking hold zapping all its electrical currents
To bloom into creations while I dream
Upon awakening those seeded thoughts
  become sewn at every seam

A tapestry of how my day now blossoms
Continuously thinking with feelings of all that I wanted
Heart penetrates its miraculous beats
Of feelings so appreciative of the thoughts I keep
Then before I realize it they have manifested
Just for me to have the experience, to add
  another memory for my soul

Then onto the next seed to implant
Nurturing them with feelings of ownership
I know when they are ready for picking
Because all doubt has dissolved,
vanished like the morning fog
Leaving me with only flowering blossomed thoughts

AnnaMarie Antoski

Chapter 2

Reflections
Of
Nature

AnnaMarie Antoski

Nature's Rhythm

What perfect paradise to observe to behold
Nature all around each and every curve
Bunnies hopping in their inspiring delight
Birds chirping they're last songs for the night
As the darkness engulfs all that was once seen
Like a veil drawn as the sunset gives its last peak
Fluttering moths hypnotized of every light
While fire flies spark their alluring so bright

Just when silence beckons the pure peacefulness of the land
Nature shows its self again
As a harmonious symphony becomes to fill the air
Of frogs in perfect unison
Like a concert for all to share
Bliss in paradise, orchestrated by nature
A sweet lullaby to all of my senses
Heart felt ecstasy expanding its unity
To the webbed perfection of natures bliss

Crystallized Reflection

Immersed in nature's beauty
Of the magnificence it does portray
From the sky's during my night sleep
To awaken to crystallized delight

Everything coated with sparkling glow
Frozen in time for me to see and appreciate
Glistening tree branches of sparkling ice
Imbued with freshly fallen snow

Such a heavenly sight
As the sun shines its rays on everything
Bright glistening sparkles everywhere I look
There's no finer beauty of creation to bestow

Feeling the fresh snow under my feet
Radiance of nature transforming from night to daylight
As I touch the icy prisms on the tree branches
I feel the warmth of my fingers melt the ice
Such moments of bliss frozen in time
Captured in my space for an infinite memory to retrieve anytime

Reminding me how we can transform anything
From beliefs of doubts can be transformed into all possibility
Melting and reforming any thought we so choose
So we can experience glistening joy
Of our divine nature of empowering sparkle and shine

*P*aradise

Such a sensual feeling that paradise can bring
  In this little space of mine
    With Christmas music playing
      And just a couple tastes of wine
        Creating me to feel so much joy
          Tingling all sensations for everything I enjoy

Our natural state of bliss's perpetually heightening
  Just like being in love
    The reminder to know that's what life is all about
      But how the ego mind likes to control
        To take us out of our paradise out of pleasures realm
          Fooling us into the sloping of Downsville again

Every beat of my heart in the rhythm of the moment
  Forever can linger surpassing all judgment
    Collapsing into a kindling kind of state
      Surpassing the rational mind
        Without heavens escape
          Calm peacefulness makes everything refined

To live and play in love's reality
  Where past and future just fades away
    Only forever's reality is the ultimate high to stay
      None of life's challenges dare enter in
        Cause that would only strip bliss away!

Only the magical, joyous memories can enter
  Endowing the cells to dance
    All that is of love that mankind needs to resurrect
      Then heaven can be more than just a moment in time

Such as magical memories trigger the bliss
  To be in the moment of the hearts beats to shine
    Crystallizing time into the spaciousness of forever
      Exalted to the extreme as paradise caress thee
        Like love dust captured the totality of me

PURE IN ETERNITY

Oh blessed one of infinity, I have finally arrived
As peaceful bliss not only surrounds me, is now beyond surreal
I feel it so whole and serene, just mellowing in all my senses
Caressed in the presence that is indescribably so real
In this moment of wholeness, connected with everything expanding into eternity
Where the illusion of magic and miracles are only a breath
Though memories of the journey seemed like a rough and struggling storm
Now I know it was worth every part to get me to here and now
Where I reside in eternity, moment by moment
Peace, love, heavenly bliss being one with it all…

I am the birds flying
I am the plane above
I am the river flowing
I am the rocks stuck in the mud
I am the wind that is fiercely blowing
I am the leaf that the winds is moving
I am the tree that is secure in the ground
I am each blade of grass that is turning green from brown
I am the dew that is wet and turning dry from the sun
I am the rainbow that was once so far
I am the others I see, hear and feel
I am all now that I have become whole in thee

In this blissful now that is now extending forever
I am light and free exactly how it was suppose to be
Returning from once I came but now wrapped in wisdoms embodiment
I feel it, I know it, and the blessing is so expansive
I am one with it all, yet as I sit here quietly
I am moving yet so still in all that I am
I am that I am, I know and feel it
I celebrate with peaceful bliss for it to last forever

The Dawning of a New Day

As I awoke to the dark black background of the night sky
Silence unwraps its serenity of the peacefulness in the early morn
Of the picturesque magnificence as the day unfolds
Oh how our Creator's signature signed in nature embedded
as a reminder for us all
That we are surely a part of it all

With the prisms of colors as the darkness fades as it lightens the sky
Engulfed of in-depth magnitude like a heart expanding unified love
The luminous beauty of the Creators creation at its best
As a reminder to be present in appreciation for all there is
Have trust that all challenges have much larger purposes
That we all have the strength to rise above it all

As we be one with nature as we choose to create each day
As the birds can trigger our memory to start the day in joy
With their chirping as they awake from their nights rest
A new day dawning with all choices we have to behold
To create it in anyway is the greatest gift that is given to Us All

Infinite Wave

As I sit by the water's edge
Mesmerized by it's infinite depth
I feel myself become one with the flowing waves
Feeling the sun's warmth penetrating through my body
As the serene water brushes against my feet
Engulfing all my senses unifying the totality of me

As I gaze along the water
out into to what seems like forever
I feel my body become so light and free
Gliding my mind past the edge of eternity
Oh how infinite my spirit really is

So free when not contained in any enslaved beliefs
Where all is really possible
Water reminds me of consciousness with it's infinite realities within
We are more then we could ever know
Our physical life is like a grain of sand on the beach
The more we expand ourselves into the unknown to know
The more we will surely become to experience and grow

RUMBLING CLOUDS

What a spectacular site, for my vision to see
Merging throughout all of my senses
Of such a circumference intertwined
Of hurling winds pushing my car against its path
Heavy rain twirling just like being in a car wash
That all one can do is ride it through

Then as I drove farther the vision I came upon
Left me breathless as I watched nature unleash
her empowering rage
Rain transformed to ice pellets
Splashing its force against my windshield
The wipers could hardly keep up as
My car drenched in nature's bosom

The wind spinning leaves,
which appeared like fallen birds onto the ground
Stumbling and flying up through the spacious air
The sky became blacken with the darkest clouds
That were moving so fast

Up heaving everything in its path
No cars around just me and the road
Blasted in natures most spectacular show

If moods of emotions were enticingly triggered
Nature releasing all that's stored inside
Viciously letting out pent up feelings
It would be like a fierce roaring anger letting out steam
Crying with genuine passion from submerged pent up emotions
Stirring and held in until it could not be sustained introverted any
longer

Whisked away in the spiraling winds
Rain mixed with snow and ice
Swirling, turning, pushing everything's a stirring
Clouds moving so fast, making me feel I am in the centre of it all
Like a bond of devotion the sky's seemed to circumference
its surroundings, and me into it

I stopped and lit a cigarette, stopping myself in this space of time of
experience
To take in all I could with my senses, ravishing in it all
With my window now down, I could feel the heavy wind blowing
the rain & ice on to me
Specks of pricks on my skin as it hurled through

The loud sound the wind was creating as it whirled and twirled its
nothingness
Yet creating so much power for such an unseen thing
Broken branches along the road
making my drive like a obstacle course
Dodging all that comes in my way
No animals to be seen, confined in hiding spots
Protected from natures release

Ah the beauty of a magnificent storm
Engulfing all of my senses to be adored
Where fear could of easily overtaken me
I felt a peace amongst it all
I felt as if I were in the eye of the storm
Watching, observing it all, like being in bliss,
a heaven of its own

Just as the beautiful magnificent prisms of sunrises and sunsets
This I must state was most spectacular
Melting me into it's environment it empowered
I realization how small and helpless we can be
When nature unleashes to balance itself in purity

Stars Shining So Bright

The sun setting while the night grows
The darken sky is showing it's glow
As the darkness paints its background
Allowing the invisible to now be visible
Popping into view
Sparkling visions to observe
Of stars and planets illuminating a grand show

As I wonder of these shining lights
What magnificence could they really be
Sparking data of other realities
Like a infinite brain, firing its electrical currents our way
Transmissions of information
Appearing for us as a heavenly sky
Yet behind the illusions veil
Could be more then we could ever know
Like a hidden doorway that leads us
To dimensions unbeknown

Dazzling Fire

Dance your rhythm as you sparkle and dazzle us
Whimsical colors interwoven flames
As you crackle with swooshing sounds so crisp to our ears
While warming our bodies when we come oh so near

How you cook our marshmallows to taste so delicious
Yet can burn us if we touch you, but we know you're not malicious
We can not embrace you, you'll not have none of that
But allow us to enjoy you in the most peaceful sense

We know our boundaries
We keep our distance
And just lavish in our perpetual resistance
In the calm serenity you exude
Keeping us mesmerized as your flames protrude

Oh Little Grasshopper

Oh little one where have you come from
and where are you going?
Hopping as you do, all adventure is so curious for you
Do you care where you go? Or do you like everything new?
Are you coming along for the ride or are you going to jump off
Now that there's nowhere for you to hide

How you hang on so tight against the windy flight
If you don't get off soon
You'll be somewhere else so far away from your home
You eyes seem to tell a story of your trusting nature
Like a natural friend that's popped up to say hello

Hold on you do with all your might
Yet my own fears perception is that you just might be in fright
So stop we do and gently nudge you to hop off
So you can continue your journey where you had left off

Playful Chipmunk

As you sit there observing knowing you are safe
Grabbing up the nuts I put out for you to take
Quite the audience you have gathered
As they watch you through the window
Yet your thoughts seem not scattered

All three cats and a bird
Sitting quietly watching so closely not to make a sound
Thrilled they are just of your presence
You stare at them as to say with a frown
Why don't you all come out to play
Probably not what's on their mind
But to me, you're just so cute
I could watch you for hours but soon you do scoot

Watch over Me

Oh how secure you make me feel
As you share your bed, it's really so cozy
I know I am safe
Look how much bigger you are then me
But when you bark, I really get startled
I know it's your way of telling me
That another is around
So I can flee and not be found

Since your on the look out
I think I will take a nap
So please don't bark at silly things like the wind
Just to startle me again

This poem I wrote was inspired by my nieces and nephews and their love for insects and nature.

The Butterfly

Into existence I became, natural to the world
I birthed and grew, though slimy
Of coarse because I am a little worm

From vibrations telepathized
What others did say that I was just a dirty thing
While they walked and took notice
As I squiggled and tried to hide
Like giants towering and heavy steps synchronized
What a challenge not to become squashed

Then one day there was a change
Though I struggled and hurt with lots of pain
Something of a metamorphosis from deep inside
Everything became so dark
This urge to push and push, I felt confused
What do I do, I don't want to die
Could it be that someone stepped on me?
This just isn't how I used to be

I struggled and pushed, no I just can't give up
Dark, why is it so dark and so much pain
Then all of a sudden I felt a squeeze then a release
And when I looked down, I seen the old me, a long worm
Lying there with no movement, only just a shell

What is this, I now have wings and I can walk along
Instead of squiggling like before
These wings are so big and lift me up
I am so light and can see so far

In each passing day, changes came my way
I heard others say as they stared
Expressing beauty and magnificence
Who Me? Is that who they are talking about?
I am still me, with a different body I shout
But they don't use the language of telepathy

One of them so gently took me in its hand
Then put me into a jar made of glass
I could not escape; I tried with all my might
I felt like a prisoner in a cage stuck inside

Oh yes they cared for me in all loving ways
Fed me and showed me to others in praise
The little one would sing me sweet songs
But as I looked past the glass so beyond

Freedom to roam and fly with the breeze
And intermingle with others, even the bees
As they dashed and flew and played with the birds
Lying on twigs and leaves, enjoying all that they pleased

My owners are nice, but owned me they did
They loved me just a little too much
Stifling my life when I wanted to roam
I did not want to be owned

I felt like I was suffocating and wanted to experience more life
They did not understand, because they could not hear my plea
Instead they were worshiping me
This just did not feel right, I was feeling so sad

One dawning of a colorful night
I watched the prism sky so bright
A moth was circling around the room
Then noticed me there and flew to my gloom
The lid was barely on the glass jar that became my caged room
The moth shot down in a towering rage
Zipped across and hit the lid of my prison cage
To the floor the lid fled

Stunned as I was, the moth screeched to come out
I followed the moth through the hole of the screen door
I did not stop to think, I just followed so excitedly to soar

Oh so free, I am free, I can fly and just be me
I am in bliss; this is just the best of the best that I could see
I guess all that wishing, hoping and daydreaming
 surely did make things come true

Later I stopped on the window seal to see if the little one was around
And I watched It was inside, but oh no,
                    water was flowing from its eyes
It was crying missing of its sweet butterfly
I heard another explain about life

When you love something set it free
If it comes back it was meant to be
never ever suffocate it by possession
To selfishly hold it just for yourself
Instead it is best to just let it be the way it wants to be
Just like you if I never let you go outside to play
You would become so sad and eventually want to run away
Love is not to be owned, love is meant to love freely

The little one dried it's tears
Sat outside plopped on the stairs
I wondered, confused of what to do
Should I go over and say hi, or ignore the little one and just fly?

The compassion I felt swelling inside
Melted the fears that was making me doubt
I flew and plunked myself by its side
It went to grab me, then pulled its hand back

And spoke these words that I will never forget
Ah beautiful butterfly, forgive me I never knew
That you had feelings and needed to bloom

Though it hurts me to let you go,
      you need your own space to grow
I love you that much, my mother tells me to let you fly
Though I just want to cry
But now I know that missing you is okay
It's all part of life, like my mother did say
Just promise me that you'll always come back,
      just to say hi and reminisce
And I promise to never hold you in capture again
We can just be forever free loving friends

AnnaMarie Antoski

Chapter 3

Magnificent

Holidays

AnnaMarie Antoski

FIREWORKS LIGHT THE SKY

Family's gathered for the first of July
The kids scream out there usual sigh
Now, is it time yet
They continuously fret
Again we explain that they have to wait
They seem doomed by their fate

They impatiently watch for the sun to set
For the sky to paint it's color black, they do know
So the fireworks can be our compass of light
That thrills our vision from exploding its surprising show
Of colored rays that light up the sky
Crackling and bursting
making the night appear like a brightened day
Then we sit by the fire
And wish upon the stars
To create the future to be all we want

The Magic of Christmas

In the caressing heart of the real spirit
Let any negative energy go
Instead align oneself with the genuine meaning
Allowing the positive spirit of Christmas to flow

Blooming into the perpetual magical present moment
Where only love, caring, hopefulness glows
Sparkle it with fun, joy and compassion, and infinite hope
Letting yourself chuckle with laughter, let your belly jiggle

Irrelevant of any dire situation
that may try to alter your glow

Let all frustrations just melt away
Perceive all and everything in a new way
In the true Christmas emotions
Whether it be December or July
Allow yourself the grandness rite to feel it all year round

Let the Christmas music vibrate your soul
Of the lyrics of power and knowing to continuously grow
Let the Christmas lights remind you of your chakra's so bright
Allowing your health to be harmonized with the
energy so aligned that's just right
In the frequency of synchronicity to manifest
all your desires
Keeping your energy bountiful and high

Choosing the genuine Christmas spirit all of the time
Will only be a blessing to one's own self
Flowing continuously within and without
As you shine like the biggest star
Of what you really are
A spiritual being in physical

The Christmas Spirit

So its Christmas time again
Well for most of the world, except for me
Because for me Christmas is everyday
December just magnifies it all, of what we should always be
The spirit, the love, the joy, fun and laughter of infinite excitement

Its all in the state of being
Being nice, being happy, being childlike, being Christ like
Being like God intended us to be
Trusting, sharing,
To create our life of perpetual joy

Its not getting pulled in to worry and frustrations
Or trying to buy everyone on your extended list
Or going broke in the process,
wearing all your patience down
Let it be easy and simple
Being creative to loosen the load, so peace can be found

Be the smile, be the laughter,
add to the love of forever after
Not for fears to reign
Instead allow love to flow
From your heart, let it swell so you can know
It's all about having fun of the greatest times

To enjoy this spirit of bliss and joy
Now and every day
Forever in this now
Reverse every frown
Back into a smile

Allow the now to extend
Each and every day in each and every way
Allow the Christmas spirit be the now eternally
Unifying all days into Christmas
Allowing life to magically expand
Bringing Christ ways in every day
To open each day like a magnificent present
Allow the love to touch upon everyone

HALLOWEEN

Spooky music playing on the radio
Kids dressed up going house to house wanting more
Treats, they take, whatever is given at the door
Tricks they can't eat, so they completely ignore

Such a excitement fills the air
With all of their laughter and funny scares
Filling their bags until they overflow
They barely can carry them, but they still want some more

As the night closes in, they are dragging their feet
Because they have to wait another whole year for more treats

PARTICLE TO WAVE

So solid it feels as I hold it in with my fingers
Particles so hard as I try to twist it but my thoughts do linger
Knowing it takes is seeing it in advance
Seeing it change to invisible moving waves
Then in a magical moment
Unlocked of space in time
It feels like hot putty
And twist and twist so fine
Till it hardens to its original hard state
That would only take physical strength to twist again
That only deceives if you want to feel reality's real flexibility

The Real Christmas Gift

All the presents sit under the tree
Bought and wrapped with such rushed tensed energies
From have to do's and deadlines to meet
How can any of those gifts be given and taken
with true sensitivity
Mostly picked with good intentions
Yet missing the mark of the real Christmas gift
The gift of the one and only Source of All
The gift of our truest reasons for being here
To connect with our Infinite Love

The Gift in You

Christmas, Christmas, sing it again
Christ in mass consciousness, we're all brethren
Awakened Christ's to become in mass population
Not to honor or obey, with harsh sacrifices
But to open the real gift of love's divine life
And celebrate the real Spirit to shine through

Giving and receiving physical gifts is nice
But the real gift, the divine secret of true life
Is the gift from the Infinite Creator's cue
Its inside me and its inside you

To open the gift that's inside you
Is to active the God gene DNA in our body to renew
Then the Christmas lights will shine so bright
From our glowing harmonized chakras
We will feel lifted and light
As we become adult Gods and Christ like
Taking all our responsibility back
To open the inner gift, encoded of the creator cell

We believe and experiment through all experiences
Of always returning to that genuine love of existence
To know thy self, through all observation
From all beliefs that eventually become knowing

The real gift of real love,
what Christ in mass is what Christmas is all about
To feel it and know it in our own hearts
Our lives is then released all our judgments are dissolved
Now we can celebrate the real gift, the only thing that matters
Nourishing the god seed, letting it bloom into Creators of Love

Easter's Renewal

Easter is the time of year
To remind us of our power within
A renewal of cleansing of negative energy
The knowing to celebrate our new beginnings

To cherish ourselves, excluding all judgments
To bask in the warmth of self honoring, without doubting
To embrace our resurrection of the powerful beings we really are
And to smile and keep ourselves in joy,
Irrelevant of any dire energy from the past we may have conjured and
exploit

Easter to me is the reminder
Believe, value, think, speak then behave in the Present Moment
where real-ly all the power will always reign
Love ourselves enough that the love flows outward
And touches everyone and thing we come in contact with

So lets be like a bunny, and hop in fun & excitement
That we are Beings of Power
And ravish our taste buds in some delicious dark chocolate
And bless ourselves through all we've all gone through
We've come above many high waters
And have such beautiful new beginnings to experience
Have a miraculous, joyous Easter, all year round

Feeling One With It All

A New Year's Beginning

I am alone, but not lonely
Through my connection with Infinite Source
I feel all presence, even though my physical eyes filter it out
I feel whispering thoughts gently making me aware

I am visible in physical but my totality is also part invisible
I am a part of you though perceived as a stranger
I love and trust you, because we are one unified
I feel the warm breeze of wind gently brushing against my skin
I know that all invisible is genuinely real to sense to know
Consisting of entities of quite the mixed variety
I know the beckoning sounds of whirling wind does urges my
awareness
I understand by feelings that vibrate in the invisible
but so real waves of forever
I used to perceive reality through conformity's perception
Until I came to know the real reality before its physical creations

I in the past was a slave to my altered ego's influence
Until my ego united its transformation with my higher natural self
I believed once in judgment, until I knew judgment separates
Now I am one with source who has no more comprehension to
separate
I just love and extend that love, as we are all one of the whole
I was once in need of conditions of the ego to be glorified

Now I sit in the most brilliant honor of the source that shines of all
The breath of life and infinity itself
Continuously breathing its breaths of giving and transforming

Love beholds no conditions, only to share and give
Life has now become a alive with great beingness
To enrich with the naturalist joys
Hail the ego that died its death, transformed courageously in uniting of
real love
Sacrificed nothing but fears expanded perception of separateness
And now is endowed of full consciousness in its embodiment
Tis the enlightened awaken evolved ones that seed the heavenly
experiences on earth

Kids Day

This I conglomerate to create it to be
A day to celebrate for all kids, no matter of age
That you are acknowledge and blessed in grace
Without any judgments, just because you had caretakers,
all flavors included, none are denied

irrelevant of challenges, your specially unique and divine
just because you had to put up with all we leashed out
this kids day is to celebrate in honoring for you
that we appreciate all you have put us through
and then all you have done that has helped us grow strong

As caretakers and parents we learn as we go
Trying to guide in the best ways we know
When we goof up, you still love us in spite
Only triggering what's in us that ignites
We remind ourselves that you are our future
And deserving of your own special day too

AnnaMarie Antoski

Mother, Father

Amaze me, you always do, oh mother
You spoke such exuberant words
When you said, this will not take you down,
You again told your body cells just what to do
Not even allowing any distrusting fear thoughts to detour what you
consciously choose
Told the sickness and rash to go away, within hours it was gone
You said, I won't feel sorry for myself
You said because you are the boss of your body cells

Father, father, you amaze me too
Always doing so much
Your helpful advice with caring voice
Lingers away even when we get off the phone
Better, better, you say it till its true
You sure have come a long way in healing
We continue to watch your healing bloom

Mother and Father united
So blessed I am to share in so much divinity
Of the two of you flourishing together
Keeping the family so connected
Experiencing all challenges transform to laughter
Always lightening the loads
Like making grey sky's blue

Blooming Spring

Rain pouring down, melting the snow away
Everyone's waiting, some even most impatiently
For spring to finally bloom,
With all its seeding ready
To show us all the signs, that spring is surely on its way

Grass now turning greener,
With every rainfall
Then as the warm sun shares its rays
Everyone keeps celebrating for more

I myself like winter too
Even though here it seems like the north pole
All the seasons are so cozy
I wouldn't change a thing
Rather just bask in it all for the joy
That every season brings

Snow is a reminder of our divine innocence,
 embedded potential to change
Autumn shows so magnificently,
 through its varieties of colors that become rearranged
Rain, hail, snow, fierce blowing winds, sunshine, blooming spring in
everything,
How blessed to have a bit of everything

AnnaMarie Antoski

Chapter 4

Flowing

Appreciation

What Heaven I Am a Part Of

As I look out our window
Miraculous nature is abound
One day a river with its flowing water
Another day its miles of fields all around
The massive stretch of natures curves
Thrust of all shapes and colors unfold to surround
Of nature in all its natural swerves

Its heavens borderline
And how magnificent it feels
Ignites such appreciation of serenity
My desires manifested with such serendipity
The land of joy
The beauty of nature
Heavens border
That I am at one with

Upon the hills where the turkeys walk
To the geese waiting to hatch their eggs
And the chirping birds singing their songs
The prancing deer grazing along
The jack rabbits even seem in tune
Such a blissful place to be
Nature revealing its secrets to me
Blessed I feel to be such a part of

In the awe of such delight
With the flow of appreciation from my heart
Knowing I am one with all this creation as I evolve
That I am one with the source that created it all
Where all is possible, all is renewed
Every second is something so brand new
Though appearing the same
It never really is
Everything changes within its minute revelations

THE GREETING OF THE CREATOR SMILING TO ME

In awake meditation, just being in the now
Eternally expanding in the blissful joy all around
The darkness of the night and silence of all sound
As hundreds of acres of land endows as it surrounds
Not a peep from the forest
Only the silent exuding stars in the dark sky
For hours I just sit in the joy of observance of it all
Sustained, uplifted, my spirit is high

As the expanding now of eternity
Allows the day to unfold
I experience the oneness of it all
As the Infinite Creator raptures its call
As if a painting is coming to life

I hear the chirping of the birds
Magnificent symphony of a multitude of different chirps
The most divine beauty to my ears
Nature awakening joyfully in harmony
As the darken sky is also unfolding
Its most exuberant colors in the horizons
It's experiencing heaven awakening to its early dawn

Describing it in physical words surely is only fractional
As it's in the feeling that can only be felt
As my heart expands with such delight
Of such grateful appreciation to experience this in physical
Embodied in my senses of the most magnificence of the infinite

Peeking and showing Itself to me
As if to express its oneness in its reflection back to me
Of being a part of it all just so naturally

Brighter and brighter it perpetually becomes
Bird's expressions of they're naturalness to it all
Colors are so brilliant and mixed of their prisms
In a giant holographic passion expressed in physical
Beauty of it breathing into my soul
In the appreciation that I am also a part of it all

THE MIRACLE OF A NEW DAY

Each day I awaken when the darkness blankets everything
I sit in the divine silence basking of its exuberance
As I feel my heart expand in love
I in my blissful state of experience
Become one with the waking morn
Of nature and the sunrise of each new day

Each new day is unique
Yes the same birds are chirping
With the beautiful colors light up the sky
But each day is always a little different
As I become one with every moment of surprise
A color changes just slightly
More illuminating to my eyes
I am aware through the divine's allowing of experience

Nothing else matters
Only this moment that expands
Of more heavenliness because I am aware
In such high vibe of appreciation
Of each new day that becomes
In each day there is another way
To be thankful for all we have

Sing joyously as the birds
Be bright as the prismy colors that radiate in the sky
My full senses bloom to reap in the miracles of it all
This surely is heaven on earth
How could it be anything else?

When we focus on the magnificence
And be grateful for everything we have

Whether little or allot
It is really in what we believe to see or not
When we become the silence and one with each new rising day
We are seeing and feeling the best there always is
And there is best in everything
Even the things that may seem of negative
When flipping the coin to the other side
You will see everything in a brand new light
And feel love and gratefulness in your heart
Because that is what we are created of

Realized Appreciation

Missing the blossoming of another brand new day
Of new inspirations, new ideas to come my way
Instead of getting out of bed
I choose to sleep in instead
The sun is already risen
Tomorrow I will be up before the crack of dawn
To experience the sunrise in another unique way
The oneness I always feel is so blessed to me
In the field of ecstasy as bliss fills the air

Like the magnificence of technology
That within a whimsical second that our thoughts
which instantaneously converts from our inner minds
to the finger tips unto the keyboard
Then transfers onto a screen page and as soon as we click
the send button it appears so many miles away onto your screen
to be received
To just stop and think about the awesomeness of how it works
Creates appreciation for our lives in how simply it's magnificent
Its when we take it all for granted
that we miss the divine beauty of it all

It's the same in almost everything we do during the day
Every technology we use is so magnificent when we take the time to
observe it that way
The magical life we get to experience
And the most amazing thing is all the technology is an outer realm
of our own capabilities of possibilities we have within

The Storms of Life

Oh how the rain pours down, purifying everything it touches
Soaking up all the negativity with its tears of love
And the lightening is a reminder of the
electrical power of our thoughts
How our thoughts can strike all possibilities when we ignite it
with repetition instead of dismissing
To empower it into becoming, just from our thoughts
The thunder is a reminder to snap us back to the greatness
of life
To startle us, to awaken us from the dark dream
of losing our divine esteem
The storm is a reminder to relax into the knowing that all is
possible
The storms of life, our ups and downs, our fury and love
Our experiences that have become as within so then without
The storm is such a reminder of the gods we all are
Creating through electrical frequencies all that we think about
The storm is comforting, to curl up and watch
The power that it instills and its all in each one of us

Love is the Key

The greatest things in life are free
Like the whirling wind that we can't see
Brushing along the tree limbs so grand
Then we see the results of its invisible hands

Invisible is all of our thoughts
Continuously thinking without realizing their results
Yet thought perpetually does attract and create
what we want & don't want, nothing stops for it to wait
In ways we can see when things synchronize throughout our days of
all we thought
We just can't deny when we observe long enough

We come to know the absolute greatest invisible is love
We can not see its energy, yet its the most powerful in it's results
Holding together liken a glue
The whole world and universe, its true
Making our heart fill with sometimes sadness and sometimes joy
Can make us cry or grin such a big smile we can't deny
Can make us high like walking on a cloud
Can melt away depression in a flick of a thought into its feeling
there's no doubt

Yes love is a powerful force that keeps us alive
Keeps us wanting that feeling to forever ride
Its a orgasm more potent then sex
It can lift us up when everything may appear that we dread

Recalling love feelings can be felt in the heart
Expanding in the chest and over flowing without

Allowing one to appreciate everything good or bad
Nothing else seems to matter when its done or thought
in genuine love.

So next time you feel scared, sad, worried or depressed
Just think of anything to do with uplifting love
Its a guarantee you will be lifted and refreshed
Your smile will extend to all that you interact with and perceive
Its a feeling that fills us with glee

So remember when you need a lift
Think of love and enjoy it's ride
Listen to Christmas music in the middle of July
Add some Christmas lights to sparkle the room
Get up a little earlier and experience the miraculous sun as it
blooms
Observe the birds chirping even though its so cold outside
Watch them playing games with the squirrels
Nothing seems to alter their bliss

The hopping rabbits on the new fallen snow
Watch the full moon light up the sky like a big light bulb
Illuminating its aura of whiteness with its glow
How the stars are sparkling on the dark background of sky
Of your breath steaming out of your mouth when its just that cold

Just remember nothing is worth robbing you of the simplicity of the
natural things
Of the impressible feeling that it does give
That is entwined in love's energy
Perpetuating everywhere
when perceived through the feeling of love
All comes alive in such a refreshed way every day

Love is the key, the glue, the feeling of the e-motion, the joy and
hope of it all
Even if its just in thought, its still felt and extended without
Love your burdens and stresses
until they melt away to give you hope

AnnaMarie Antoski

Long enough till everything
is so humorous, cozy and okay when surrendered to love

That's love, that
That's the energy of what its all about
That's what its there for, reminders of the high to be perpetually felt
To transform anything that brings us down into a heavenly feeling
One simple thought can change our perception of everything
Just like that, like a flick of a switch, in our mind from our thoughts
So bask in love thoughts so it can be felt extended throughout
Its vibration will radiate and brush against space and time
Effecting all that you perceive,
just like a dream that feels so real
when you wake up

OUT OF ROBOTIC, *INTO AWARENESS*

Of all that I know
 There's always something new
  To learn and evolve to grow and renew
   Like habitual daily routines that become so stale
    That we do just because it became a habit we follow
     That leads us to robotic motions that are so frail
      Into new actions that then do unfold
       Our hearts will flourish to expand
        As it lets go of its tightened hold

Each time we change our daily routines
 Do something different to snap out of all that just seems
  Habitual things we do every day without a care
   So we can become to be more aware
    All the while it's also changing our wiring of our brain
     Creating more spontaneity of adventures that we can proclaim
      That may even lead us in a different direction
       Then we can notice many more surprises
        and let go of all the idea's of perfection
         Like appreciating so many things we have missed
          Just because we broke free from the things
           we think we must do that we put on our lists

Appreciating the person who picks up our trash
 And the swirling bees that we all need while we live on their land
  The trees that gives us our oxygen for each breath we take
   When was the last time you told a tree thank you
    and touched them with your loving hands?
     Or felt the morning dew on your feet
      Or responded back to the chirping bird
       With your own creative chirpy song?
        To keep stirring sweet harmony along

AnnaMarie Antoski

Chapter 5

BLESSED
IS
FAMILY &
FRIENDS

HAPPY FATHERS DAY DAD

When I was younger I do recall
I would write in your cards
 The Best Father of them all
That was so many decades ago and still the same is still true

When we need a listening ear, you are there to listen
And give your opinion and best advice from your experiences
You are there when we need some comfort
You always share with empathy
You love us all so unconditionally
You teach us through example, you do walk your talk
Everything you do is from your caring loving heart

Words really cannot convey, all we really want to say
There is nothing that could ever compare
        of the LOVE that you do share!

We are so blessed to have you as a Dad
You are the hub of our family's wheel
You smile when you had so many challenges
You laughed when stresses were so great
You loved when we were so rebellious
You hung on just knowing and believing
        one day we would see the light

Though we all had differences of opinions
Emends were always reconciled by night
Because dear Dad you shine your love so bright
the light of your heart always shining for us
Illuminating your rays through all of our detours
Thank you for shining your beacon of love

On this father's day,
it gives us another opportunity to express
our thanks and love
In our appreciation for all you have been
 and continue to always be and do
Thanks for being who you are
May miracles pop into your life to surprise you every day
May you inhale the Universal Love you deserve
And exhale any debris to be purged
So that your lungs can become one day soon,
so renewed of the breath of love that is deserving for you

Happy Anniversary Mom and Dad

Over fifty decades ago the two of you made your vows
To stay together through heavenly days
And even when the challenges of the worst came about
You together take it all in stride
    and have the faith to know it will all work out
Keeping not only the two of you together
        but also the whole family
    that you both have created since your marriage vows

Raising five kids,
and all of our friends that keep changing thru the years
The two of you always accept, allow and openly invite
All who come upon your door
No matter if it's day or night
Whether for fun or helping others
The two of you have an kind open heart

That's the very reason many look upon you as family
Because you accept everyone with never a prejudice
But love with no conditions

Dedicated commitment of enduring bond of love
For a marriage to stay together as long as the two of you have
Through thick and thin you'd made it through
Not only all of us kids and our friends and mates
    but many generations of grandchildren too

Such a role modeling you both are of how a marriage should be
To still laugh and keep every moment precious
Yep, that's our Mom and Dad!

MASTER PARENTS OF LOVE

HAPPY PARENTS DAY

Mom and Dad you both have lead the way
Always in what you do and say
Role modeling of unconditional accepting love
Not just for a few but for everyone you both encounter of

We learned compassion and sweet empathy
To share and express smiles of kindness in all we be
Through challenging and good times you share so free
A love then never sways or hinders
We wish you miraculous days to always unfold
Filled with all your dreams to be fulfilled for the two of you
On this special parents day to behold

Happy Anniversary to My In-Laws of Love

Though I was a stranger when I came into your sons life
You greeted and accept me into your family with such delight
All through the years as the family expanded with every new face
You both continued caring and giving with such grace
Released of any judgments that could of perpetually lingered
Forgiveness was what you both naturally engendered

All the stories I heard of your family's past
Filled me with compassion and laughter
While amazing me with the strong family's bond
Sparking your love as if it was a family song
Absent time away never lead the family astray
Enduring accepting love
   is what you both have always shown in every way

Feels so right as we visit and talk into the night
Such comfort you both allude
In all we do go through
In laws of the greatest kind
Flourishing each day as you both extend your bonding love
Sustain and evolve in your matrimony bond

AnnaMarie Antoski

Happy Birthday to You,

My Dear Mother in Law

Birthdays have not meant much to me
In the past few years that I've decided to be free
Free of the labeling that the numbers decline me to be
Or maybe having such a young superstar as a mate
Made me want to stop and save some youthful grace

Whatever my reasons, I know it's not the norm
However because you are so special to me
I had to acknowledge this day to be adorned .
Because since the first time that we met
There was a kinship of bonding that I could never deny
It was from the start and has grown into my life

It reminds me of a beach, our friendship is like the sand
The grains are so infinite
when it appears to be gone from the flow of water
Underneath the sand goes on forever
Just as I feel of our friendship of us together

That is what you have become to mean to me
A mother-in-law, a sister, a confidant, a healer
Listening with compassion spiced with genuine empathy
Whenever I am over burden, you are always there to make things better

I see so many qualities that your son inherited from you
Of caring and compassion

with such a loving pure essence always renewed
These special qualities are bonded from a mother
Even through challenging times, he can make me laugh and smile

And make me feel special,
Just as you always do.,
        sometimes tears from the hysterics of laughter

When everything seems so doomed and stuck
You will say something funny and I forget what I was worried about
There was a connection that is rare to find
I am so lucky to have found it with you, without any doubt
You are an incredible genuine soul,
        I wish all your dreams to one day all come true
So that you can bask in pure blissfulness,
        of a life that feels like heaven for you

I am so fortunate to have become into a family as yours
To feel so comfortable with a mother & father in laws as yourselves
To have so much in common and feel as a part of your family

I am just sitting here, letting whatever comes from my heart
So easily of memories does the release of words cometh pouring out
When things surface so deep, the emotions stir like water falls
The release in writing feels so freeing
Especially when it's genuinely pure with all its true meaning

 So to you... birthday girl, whatever your day may become
Keeps your smile glistening, because you're a special mother in law

AnnaMarie Antoski

EXTRAORDINAIRE
BIRTHDAY TO YOU

Birthdays come and birthdays go
  Year after year, a notch of one more
    Since you're still so young with so much life ahead to experience
      What I hope for you now, is that each and every day forward
Is blessed with a lucky streak of abundance for you to reap

Filled with excitement and days of fun
  Wishing that all stresses will one day will be all gone
    Like a river that flows, may your days overflow with purity of love
      And that every single one of your desired wishes
All manifest to you one by one

Hope today is a greater day for you
  Even through these challenging times you are going through
    I send blessed wishes of energy for you to receive
      That all can just be more than fine
Everything for you can be magnificently extraordinaire

Happy Mother's Day

Whatever your day may turn out to be
You are like the tap of love that flows
To acknowledge that you are thought of today
Of all your infinite hours and days
As you continuously be the bearer of a mother's traits

Motherhood, the most exhausting job
No one can ever know unless they do the walk
And you have done such a great job
Starting out so young with a child and on your own
Now with two and a mate to go along

As a mother I would like to say
Congratulations on this day
You've created life in the one's you have birthed
And kept it all going, through all the struggles you've endured
Celebrate this day as best as you can
Even if it's just a hot bath or hot tea in your hand
Do something that's just for you

It may seem forever in the so distant future
But it will surely come, that I do know
That your beautiful children will grow to adults
Then all the gratification will show its worth
Through empathy they will know
The bonds of a mother with their children
That makes everything of the chores of today
Be so worth it in every single way

KINDSHIP OF SOULSHIP

Life is so amazing, once upon a time, strangers we were
Unbeknown to us, of what each other truly was
Just people in this world, doing our own things
Then somehow our paths met
Whether destiny or fate
Altering a part of our lives
We have become soulship friends
I treasure through the years

Able to pour our troubles and hearts desires
With no concerns or any judgments
Releasing conditions, cares and doubts
We just release feelings held in then let out
Whether through tears of joy, laughter or tears of fear or sadness
A once upon a time stranger has now become a soulship friend

Though sometimes days and weeks may pass
With only conversing through emails that our received and sent
Sometimes not spoken to for weeks
But time is so irrelevant at the soul level
The once upon stranger has become heart felt
A connection, a bond, a confidante
Someone cared about from the deepest depths of thy heart
Entwined like a thread, connection was webbed
Like a tapestry of art, it became from the start

Time becomes a no thing, when it is from the soul
Always able to take up, like no time has ever passed
That is friendships made in Heaven
Probably in blueprint before birth on this planet
Nothing seems to sever any of our connections

Cause the threads were sewn with pure love's perfection

Forgiveness is always instantaneous
 Caring surpasses any negatives
   Time becomes infinite
    Like a song and dance of our spirit and soul
      Being of no effort, just unconditional
That is truly what our friendship, kinship into soulship is for me

SISTERLY LOVE

Sister's from birth yet we're like best friends
Having our challenges we never pretend
When we have our hurts
Always with open hearts we let it all out

Precious you are, it's a rhythm from my heart
Through all we endured separate and together
We always felt genuine love of empathy
Giving and sharing from small tots to adults
Nothing ever altered our sisterly bond of love

An angle is what you are to me
That will never change
You are a true virtue of grace
It sure does shine through in all you do
And everyone you ever encounter and meet

Best of all you see the love in others
Role modeling how all can be
No matter what any other does judge
You bring chaos back to harmony

Our sisterly love can surpass the tests of time
Uniquely special you will always be
And thanks for always bringing the best out in me
It lifts my heart to feel so free

Miraculous Sons

What really could I ever say
 To express what the two of you mean to me
  Words surely can not describe what I feel so deep from my heart
   The love that the two of you have perpetually shown
    That never wavers to alter of what I do or become
     The two of you are like a love source of infinite peace
That warms my heart and soul and never wavers to cease

I blessedly appreciate my miraculous sons
 With love from the deepest realms of my heart
  From little babes you've always found your way
   Never losing sight of allowing, accepting of love's rays
    The many long roads we took together
     Imprinted in our memories to find
      The best of the best of all we went through
       Just because I've been blessed with the ultimate best kind
Two sons that live everyday in every way of unconditional love

Challenges were only tests of time
 You both use them to shine
  Being who you both are birthed to this world
   Made my life always feel so divine

Neighbors of a Special Kind

I'll never forget the first day we met
Feeling like family,
no one would thought we were strangers
Seems like we've known each other for years

So many similarities
The two of you welcomed us so generously
As we spoke so openly
Holding nothing inside

Just pure fun and laughter
Sharing and so caring
As we talked and did wonder
Why it took us so long to finally meet
A great friendship that will always expand deeply

Comfort we felt
As soon as we became in your presence
The two of you will always be in our hearts
Of the friendship that bonded
To never be altered

Though days go by so fast
We know in an instant
When we get back together
It will always be like time never did pass

My Precious
Daughter's in Laws

You both are uniquely special
My heart has always resonated harmonious love
Like daughters to me right from the start
You both extend compassion with generous hearts

All judgments you both push aside
It's the caring you both exude
How both of you perfectly extended into our families
Like a woven familiarity
That keeps the bonds intertwined
Time may pass by so quick
But it never alters the love that the two of you express

Your personalities shine a prism
That seem so unique yet different
Together we always find
That we are all so one of a kind

As the years go by
More in love with you both I find
Appreciation that I am so blessed to have the very best
Daughters-in-love, as law does not do it justice
Of the beauty you both radiate and shine

Brothers Uniquely Divine

I have three brothers so divine
Each one is uniquely of a different kind
Of personalities that flavor our lives
Rainbow of grace when we all get together
The fun is priceless and precious
Each brother is like a unique flower
Each one extends their bond of enhanced family love

Uniquely the three of you mean so much to me
Bonded of a blueprint from eternity
We can talk and laugh and share what's going on in our lives
And when anyone needs help
Any of you three are there in a heart beat, extending of yourselves

How blessed am I with my loving family
Each brother expanded with my sisters in laws
That all feel like sisters to me
They have attracted the greatest
Together we are like a prism
Shining our own different ways
Yet harmonious as though we are one

Infinite Friends

Friends can only be described
 as true light that shines on the darkest nights
Absence never changes a thing
It seems we can start where we last left off
Even if its been many years
The seed became planted at first meeting it seems
And keeps blooming new buds irrelevant of the seasons that pass
Even though we experience it to go by so fast

We are webbed through all of time
With our precious memories
Fun and laughter, tears of sadness and joy
Failures and successes, with open hearts we can express
Always feeling safe and secure
Through all our experiences that we do endure

Yet through it all time never passes
Instead friendships extend forever after
Into a tapestry of no conditions of friendships love
Smiling with excitement when we get together
Our bonds of friendship love pass all tests of time

Neighbors of the Heart

There is a family that lives close by
Who were strangers to us and now friends of the heart
Within only a few short months
we have become blessed to come to know
Such a loving, caring, compassionate family
Who treats everyone special as if one of they're own

Miraculous it sure does feel to be this blessed
To know such a loving family who really does care
Words cannot describe the gratitude and appreciation we feel
For all you have done for us through these challenging winters

The heart felt emotions that all of you are always concerned
Is a divine intervention of the loving family you are to this world

A new family arose for us to bring such faith and hope back
To sustain the credibility of the loving nature of the country
We give thanks to you all for all you have done
We feel blessed that you do God's work
Expanding such love and faith for others to become

Our Loved Ones Live On

When a loved one has passed from this physical reality
So many weep great tears of their passing
Missing the physical life we all shared
Yet in our hearts we know all we can bare
Of the sadness to transform for us to have the faith to know
That these physical bodies are not really our home

We come from an infinite realm
Yet become so attached to our bodies
With rainbow of personalities that we live like a film
Some believing the show's done when death comes around
In our souls we know that's a lie
We live on eternally when we open our spiritual eyes

Our loved ones do communicate
But most are too busy in grief
To hear and feel the call
Of our loved ones voices so brief
All it takes is to quiet the rambling mind to hear
What our loved ones express to us that they are still near

Wipe away the tears with knowledge of eternal life
Then you can be so happy again
Knowing our loved ones still love
With even greater wisdom then they left this world of

Uncles and Aunts

When I think of my uncles and aunts
Such a smile becomes of memories we share
Of past and present times
That we all get together and celebrate
Family gatherings we just can't wait
To experience such laughter and fun
Grown cousins and their mates
With children now
Oh how the family tree has grown
Nothing can ever compare
When we all come together
None being left out
How the magnetism stretches far in the air
With all the laughter that echo's so far
Rumbling as we share our great love

To All Mothers
Happy Wonderful
Mothers Day

Happy wonderful mother's day
For all you are and always do
May this day be filled with fun, joy and love
For all the years that you have given,
cared, loved unconditionally, helped and nurtured
Even when sometimes it all became so challenging,
you extended yourself over and over again...

Mother's day is that reminder that is was always worth it
As our blessed children have now become our mentors,
Bonded with such angelic love that is enduring forever...

May you have the
greatest wonderful happy mother's day
Today because you are always so worth it
as you continue to touch
everyone with your unconditional love
with your hearts...

Miraculous
Mother's Day
Mom

From the day of my birth
As you held me in your arms
Indeed the journey has been so long
From baby, teenager then adult
The love and care that you always shared
Christened me with strength to endure
All that came my way with faith
As you always reminded me to let it all go

When absence filled some days to weeks
Time never passed
I know it will be that way for eternity

You smiling ways that you take care of all that you do
Never altering you from the family that grew
How your name resembles you
As a Rose you share you loving beauty with all
Blooming and caring while perpetually mentoring

From your daughter with eternal love
May all your days be blessed
With miracles and laughter
And best of everything from the Infinite God

Beautiful Radiance of Sparkles from our Hearts

Two beautiful individuals who became to be
Another part of our expanded family
Though you both are unique
 in your own amazing gracious ways
There's was never a doubt that you both would wed
Adding to both my sons lives so unified intermingling love webbed

All through the years and all that we have gone through
Not one thing has changed in the love that I feel for the two of you
Never altering of your accepting unconditional love
For me I truly knew it was always meant to be
Right from the start it was love that flowed from our hearts

Graciously Preserved

Both of you I birthed, you came through my physical body
From an eternal world that we all were before this earth
Past lives that we have experienced, we see it flickering
As passing memories we sometimes recall

I never owned or possessed to control either of you
Intuitively I knew it unfolded from an infinite plan review
My body was only a physical way
 for both your entering back into the physical haze
To continue in this earthly journey
Where we have all left off, knowing we would all return
To complete more things left undone to renew

You both have taught me intensively
And still to this day generously both in your own ways
Extend love that is so preciously created from eternal love
Appreciation that I feel is just a speck to be described
Of all that you both have done for me throughout my life

Finally Connections Received

You birthed through me, circumstances were profound
Yet I always knew that one day we would be found
So we could connect the genetic codes of our bodies and hearts
Of an enduring longing that has now been completed
Just so that all wonderings are now just footprints in the sand

So young I was when dire situation became to be
It was as we lived and learned and grew in spirituality
That many answers became to you and me
Of a much bigger blueprinted plan that became sewn in eternity

Though at birth we were greatly separated
Left in confused wonderings of many delusions
Yet every day I would think of you
Now I do see that it was truly all meant to be
As you have come through as your adopted mother's father
To continue where you had once left off

Even irrelevant of all of this
The most magnificence is that we finally met
No more perpetual wonderings of who the other is or was
Now that we have met our hearts can soar
Though you are so far away
Telepathy is the greatest of ability we have already confirmed
We know that physical is only a testing of a kind
That relinquishes all we spiritual know and do find
As we continue to grow much more openly
Whether we reconnect in physical again
Really doesn't matter now that we have rekindled the bond
It will always be eternal for us as our rhythm of our spiritual song

CELEBRATION TO YOU

Joyous spontaneous Day to You
Just because you continually renew
Yourself from the old to the bold
Creating each day to be the adventure you want to unfold

This can be such a fantastic day
When you look in the mirror with heartfelt words you say
You are a magnificent being in all that you are
Nothing has to alter your bliss when you know who you are

A creator creating each day of your own reflection
When you awaken to your extra sensory perception
Perceiving yourself in the greatness you already possess
When you just be your most natural self that you caress

Then all you see in the world will be
All you expect just because you are free
No longer caring of any negativity
You're just so ecstatically blessed
that you are your own serenity

No longer does the outside feel like a prison
Everything lights up in a heavenly prism
Knowing that all you ever perceived
Was your own filtered perception
That taught you all your returning to your own lessons
You are now free to be all you wanted to be
Your natural self that's been surging to reflect
Becomes the mirror in all that you see

AnnaMarie Antoski

.

Chapter 6

LOVERS

AND

LOVE

LIGHT THE WAY

Feeling Christmassy Love

Tis the time to be aligned
With the seasons blissful time
Spirits are roaring with such glee
And so my darling, feelings feel so free

To express such joy and love
Of all the special times from thy heart
Cherishing them like they're still real
Because in my memory your spirit's still here

Virtuously tingling deeply inside me
Like a string of Christmas lights
Sparking my inners with delight
In such a way that it illuminates me

Sensational feelings warming me
Inside and outwards, oh it's still tingling
With gleeful persuasion mingling
Of dancing emotions spurring me on of your intense love

Perpetual Heart

Oh a sweet love that never wavers
Perpetual heart forever lingers
Into the horizon of absence drawn
With greatest desires, it won't be long

Oh how our love endures the challenges of time
Encompassing all our lives wobblingly intertwined
To someday format the eternal blueprints
That is etched in our soul's design as imprints to define

Paradoxes paradise, submerged with such residue
Of enchanting memories that are forever made new
Relinquished passion created from past lives of time
Into a chaos of this world we were born
of the remembrance of a fine line

Always with hope to rekindle the plan
That ferments endlessly into the mysteries at hand
Of prisms of consciousness only tingles its way through
To one day create a rainbow that sparkles of our hue

What urging fears prelude such absence
Always struggling to release, but never pretentious
Of an undying urge that continuously surges
Magical magnetism radiating through gravitational curvatures

With impulsive instinct to look to the sky
On a black darken night, when all shows to shine
To observe the exploding lights protrude their array
Of magical brilliance sparking stars imploding in their way

This surely must be created from our energy of mysterious love
Penetrating vibrations tickling through the universe above
Electrically such fantastic surges
Such power is yet be known
But we know so deep down inside
That's how the sparkling stars are surely born

WHEN I THINK OF YOU

In the moonlight night when all is darkened yet lit with the sky light
I think of you...
When the snow in its white sparkling dance falls upon my face
I think of you...
When the falling of rain falls upon my window pane
I think of you...
When the hot summery day, sun blazing its melt, making me sweat
I think of you...
When the warm summery nights breeze, gently brushes against my
skin
Giving me goose bumps without and within
I think of you...
When i pull my blankets on to me, getting cozy and all cuddly
I think of you...
When a movie resembles our love and tears run down thy face and
into my mouth
I was thinking of you...
When the brilliant sun is setting,
allowing my eyes to see its beauty of prisms of color
I think of you...
When I stare upon the big bright moon
and I desire fly up and sit upon it
I think of you...
When I'm staring into space, out from the worldly pace
I think of you...
When I want to be caressed, with the gentleness of the best
Oh how I think of you...
Then it truly makes me wonder, I do ponder
When don't I think of you?

Then it does make me wonder
Of the reasons of so much thinking of you
Could it be no real mystery but because we never see
Such absence makes the heart fonder
And that is something we always are,
making thoughts longing longer
Absent from one another,
which triggers the missing of interactions
Or is it the attraction
Well I know there's no denying
Cause how could I hide the lying
If these words just poured out
There must be a rational fantasy
To bridge the curiosity
To allow our thoughts to just run free
Amidst the grander things of it all

LOVE SHEDS SOME LIGHT

Brand new love always creates this high
But if old pasts are not resolved, we both will sigh
Of conflicting challenges that we bring in the mix
We already know of all these relationship tricks

I am feeling a bit nervous, as I know we're in rebound
Even though this ecstatic feeling in being with you I found
Commit I know is not the thing we should do
There's too much baggage we both need to sift through

This wondrous feeling is really coming from lust
We need time from this past stuff, we need to adjust
Then to become hurt in some following time
We need to discuss this before it slips out of line
Or both come to an agreement
We're just having fun
Eliminated of concerns either will be the one

So then off we go to enjoy this exuberant ride
Of bliss till we feel it subside
Then we'll discuss any adverse challenges that may come
And still be free as a bird to follow our own shining sun

Freedom is a miraculous thing
Omnipotent its energy as it sings
That love has no boundaries; it's so free in its thrust
All we can do is have exceptional trust
It's a newer wave then the normal take
It is what I am all about and what I forsake
Sovereignty, love and freedom are surely intermittent
Hold on to your head, as it may spin a bit
Into a newer dimension of love's intervention

You Will Always Be a Part of Me

There was a time when fear lead my way
insecure that you may stray
leaving me lonely like the foggy mist
that made me see with cloudy vision
Then the sun shone through
   and the mist fell away
I know you will always be a part of me
   like the clouds in the sky
yet above those clouds all is clear
gone of perception,
only love leads my way in clarity I see

Now I can let go, like the rain stopped that day
pouring it did, like my tears when you left
I am stronger now and learned from the pain
I found my fractured self and agony I no longer kept
now I can shine and know all was meant to be
through it all I've returned to genuine love of me

You taught me so much
from the opportunity I did grow
I can wonder through the silence
and feel so secure in any flow
in the knowing it was me I had to love first
now I can extend love instead of falling into the curse
I realized falling in love can be ego based
that kept me spinning in quick sandy ground of thoughts
 Now I see it all unconditional
genuine from my heart, where all love must surely start

DIMENSIONAL CONNECTIONS

Though you're gone, passed from this plane
I do miss you and wish you were here
Mystery has become knowledge for me
of everything you always spoke about to see
I treasure it now as golden wisdom of our soul
death of an embodiment is just another dimension
  we connect with, allowing nothing to alter spiritual love

You have ultimate freedom, no heavy physical restrictions
I blow you a kiss and its caressed
  in the winds of dimensional space
Though you may not feel it with emotional senses
energy waves penetrates through all dimensions
Just as telepathy we proved in all the experiments we did
when you were here in physical

I feel what you are pondering
You want to come back
desiring embodiment again
I'm not going to be the vessel for that
But whoever you travel through, I will know that's its you
But do take your time, enjoy your stay
You know when you get too enmeshed in the desire
before you know it, you'll be back in the physical plane
  taking the wild journey of starting all over again

TICKLING MY HEART

In a whisper I can hear your voice
through the blowing wind, I can feel your touch
In the spacious garden of love, you are the key
In the moment of forever, you became my plea

Caressed in the soft vibration of you,
all disharmony melts away
In your eyes I get lost in a timeless array
    of loving warmth that you whimsically generate
In your arms I just let go
of every forever we flow

Love as you is unified in the eternal,
 shining magnetism flourishing bright
Just like stars shining through the night,
This is love's beam guiding us along

A treasure you are that keeps on shining
A present I can unwrap for the rest of time
Filled with surprises that truly do burst
Making life so blissful on this earth

Imprinted Remembrance

A swish of desire, to light my fire
  Of caressing stimulation to accelerate my conviction
    Lusting in the moment of a perpetual overflow
That seems to last forever when it comes to you!

Oh yes just nestle in my arms
  So we can rapture in a vibration that will take us to forever
   It's the magical moments of recollection memories
    Of all past times and future ones webbed of infinity
That wisps us away into a twilight ecstasy

Oh sweet lover, making all thoughts so blissful
  Take me into the starry zone for that's where it always goes
   Captivating relationship, that makes not much sense to most
    That can last and become so heightened
      So irrelevant of elongate of time passes
        High in bliss for the duration of any thoughts of it
          Never enduring, only of enjoying
The rapture of imprinted remembrance through time

Having Loved in Heaven
It Never Ends

To have loved you allowed me to remember
Gratefulness became all I appreciate
So much we did unfold
That we would never have known
Now the pain is setting in
and is when our realizing journey begins
The truest past will always know
The love that seeded surely grows

To regret will only bring more pain
To realize and know this had to be
For us to be this intertwined
Is in our memory for eternity we will find
What happens now is up to us
To carry on and fulfill our dreams
To chalk everything in our memories
And let it grow in joy and bliss
Of loves petals through all of this

You will always be to me
We loved in heaven and it extended into time and space
Anytime we think of each other
We will be connected to one another
Through thought and love is where it begins and extends
Other dimensions we have captured in our hearts lens
Live and love as we go to more experience

Nothing ends when in memory
This grain of life in physicality
Its all in the infinite schemes of things

Eternity's Natural State

How sparkling and white the snow is glistening
As the bright sun shines its rays
Slowly with its radiating warmth, melting thin layers away
Into clear water dripping down
Then as the dark night sets in, it freezes and just hangs, tis the icicles
are formed

Oh hark the beauty of nature
So a liken sensual transmutations, the building up of sensual energy
Of warm eruptions of intenseness inside the body trembles
In the imaginative indulgence of desiring climatic sensations
My body devotes its focus on its pleasurable formation

Just like every desire, such pleasure is in the heightening of awaiting
and getting there
Because of the memory of knowing the magnificent feeling of
finally letting go
and delving allusively into the phenomenal orgasm of final release
Oh such heaven, a reminder of dying and being in forever of eternity
Though in physical form, its just like a grain of sand on the beach
Just a glimpse we get when we burst the few seconds of the ultimate
rapture of blissful orgasm
Into the magical eternity of forever
Just enough to keep us wanting it again and again

SCIENCE REVEALS WHAT
ORGASM ALWAYS
SHOWED

To observe is to change just by observing
It's an act within itself
Just as in orgasm we can be split apart
From a solid physical self into a wave
That takes us into an expanded state
To experience that we are surely more then we perceive

Like a photon of light
Can be change its properties from particle to wave
We become the same when we let go and release
From one state to another
So many may miss what was always there to see
That we do it every time we allow orgasm to be

The higher we go, the more we do feel
Ecstatical states is natures natural way
Joined in a oneness that heaven can show
Bit by bit are sensory apparatus becomes to abyss
From a solid particle of being
Into a spiraling wave we become
Into our own quantified orgasmic state…

Orgasm Shows The Way

So expanded relaxed in the flow
 Of sensual pleasure caressing me so
  Into a world of pure ecstasy
   My body is trembling like bliss has finally found me

The journey to get to the one final point
 Prepping, seducing through every single thought
  Leading up to the moment to release
   Then just as I let go the feeling in extreme envelopes me

Into a magical space in time
 Where nothing else matter but this feeling so mine
  Taking me deep into a void so free
   Everything pulsing, contracting, electrical currents sparking
    Into a magical release of heavens experience

This surely must be showing me heaven
 Though only for such a short moment in time
  Leaving me wanting more of this magnificence
   The message became so clearly defined

This is a taste of heavenly bliss in the most ecstatic state
 To feel it is to know it to own it forever
  Like rolling in sparkling magical dust
   Sparking every bodily nerve to ignite to explode
    Into the void of eternity as a reminder of what we can be forever more

When we expand our self to curiosity
 To look into the future world filled through luminosity
  Of what we will become in our Divine Blossoming
   Just from the tantalizing spiral of heavenly orgasm

THE KEY TO HEAVEN
OUR
NATURAL DESTINY REVEALED

Oh blessed blissful orgasm take me away
Into the place where I love to stay
Heavenly state with no thought or doubts
Just the basking in eternity's love
Where limited descriptions won't be found
Just the blossoming of forever's map we will behold

Attachments of what I thought love was is no longer true
Love has nothing to do with all I once thought and valued to be true
Limits have been blown away to never return
Now that I have basked in ecstasy of orgasm home
The paradise all along has always been there to know
Not for a few moments but forever to grow

All unseen things have the most powerful states
The wind is a non thing yet shows itself with its force
                              and howling sounds it forsakes
Time also a non thing yet has enslave most to struggle
Bending it as much as humanly possible
Love a non thing yet humanity can twist into conditions
Into anything they want without knowing its true natures ambition
Heaven most long for
        but it escapes them like grains of sand in they're hands
Because all things that are non things are the most powerful to man

Orgasm is fleeting in the release of sexual acts
Yet it is the key to unlock the door from the past
To knowing the experience is a reminder of what could be
From just a moment of experience its power is intoxicating

Always to come back for more for us of what we can be

When orgasm is expanded into our daily lives
We find heaven in all we see and do just for its prize
Of the feelings that can sustain us throughout our days
When we come to know of orgasms maze
We bring heaven when we realize
That heaven is what we have just become
We are then heaven and love in our orgasmic self
And radiate it while we live in our paradise on earth
                    in physical orgasmic tantalized from all that we felt
We are the kingdom of heaven that orgasm has birthed

UNVEIL THE MYSTERY'S
BY BASKING IN IT

To know the unknown is to expand ourselves enough
Unweaving the mystery's of our own infinite self
Where magic keeps us spell bound
Into a mystery of unknown
Once we bask in it for more then awhile
We start to let the mystery unfold

What we find is a magical place
That magic really cannot define
Where everything is just released
To allow us many secrets left to hide
Of a state of ecstasy to expand our minds
Into pure letting go

So much lingers when we expand of the feelings
To get to know
Where all questions are answered
All knowledge turns to wisdom
From every experience that widens our perception
Into a perceptual of unlimited realities
Where all possibilities stir, waiting to be found

So bask in it longer
Until longer becomes natural
Until all wavering mundane life
Can never compare to this intertwined ecstatic state
The longer we stay in it
The more we develop our heavenliness
And nothing not anyone can alter our orgasmic love...

Orgasmic Beings of Love
is What We Are

Oh what bright shining eyes you have
 they say it's the window to the soul
Oh what a fun laugh you have, they say its exercise for the spirit
Oh what an inviting smile you have,
 they say it's your magnetism sparking
Oh what a loving feeling you radiate,
  they say that is the real you coming through
Oh what a unique way you have in being your
    infinite real self to this world

In the mirror you see
A fragment of who you really are
The face you see is only a minute reflection
 Behind the reflection deeper
All this fluctuating energy flowing
   to make and sustain the body appearance
From your senses you protrude
 Only of what you expect to be and see
Yet deeper down there is a bigger part
 deeper to where you are truly connected
 To the infinite Creator that Be

So magnificent that heaven has shown
 Through the best feeling orgasm bloomed
From the infinity we all surely came
 Finding the key to unlocking universal secrets
 To allow it's wisdom expand to know

I felt it, I know it, in that infinite state
Of oneness, of a love that is grander then the conditional life
Grander then physical could ever recite
Where everyone perpetually goes to feel
And we can bring it into everything we are and do
Expanding, evolving it to know it what we are
We are orgasmic beings so overfilling in overflow with pure love

Orgasm Shows us the
Instructions for Creating

Oh I feel it, take me higher, higher then I've even gone before
To that state where everything just is and I never ask for more
Its all there nothing can compare,
      it just is a realm that tantalizes my soul
From heavens depths I am caressed so intimately forever more
Till it is gone in that scrumptious moment faded away
Is where the desire to revisit where more comes into play
Because that place, divinely state, is the highest I have ever felt

When released, letting go that it spirals into bliss
Just as creating becomes manifested
When we let it go in its release
Is then when we sit in receivership to know
It will surely come
The pleasure is so wrapped up in the release of letting go

Instructed from bliss's orgasm
That the orgasm in not in the foreplay
It is in the release that the pleasure is felt
Just as in knowing what we desire
As we let go and release it from spirit
That it then manifests into physical
Where it can be genuinely felt…

AnnaMarie Antoski

ROUND AND ROUND WE GO

Round and round and round we go
If we do not stop then where will we go
Into a spin that keeps us in our muck
Of what we know we surely do not want

So slyly we can fall if we are not aware
Of the thinking we are doing when things don't go our way
We use blame for a few moments and then it creates the spin
Next thing we realize we feel doomed and all hope fades away

Resisting our opportunity
Stressing out our body with old thoughts
That kept the addiction to old emotions
That we once thought we were not

Popping back into show us
That we still have some fine tuning work to do
To get us to that finer channel
That orgasmic living can surely do

Believing it cannot be us
That keeps creating this chaos
However until if we keep returning to our own self
Is when we will clearly see it was all from thee

YOU ARE THE ONE

If we knew who we really were
We'd never cry in depressed fear or doubt
We'd rejoice in our capabilities
That the Infinite has always waited for us to allow
Into a world of freedom and sovereignty
Into a love so graced with magnificence
Removed from all tainted beliefs
You'd know who you really are

To look in the mirror and feel for our own hearts
That we are the creator looking at our self
Regardless of what any other limits have taught
They were only clouded thoughts
That blocked the sun from our real love
That has been always there awaiting for us
Love has carried us through time and space
Eternally is have been
All we had to do was look within
To know who we really are

Love Creators in physical bodily clothes
Trying to shine when such clouds kept us in the fog
As you smile in the mirror
And feel that you now know
It is only when you smile first
That the mirror will reflect it back
Just as the creators love
Was awaiting for you to own by knowing
That you were heaven all along

Blossoming Love

All through the years
You have been for me
Lovers, best friends, soul mates, confidant,
 even sometimes we may seem like enemies
Yet through it all, we have always found
The deeper love that surpasses all challenges
Bonding us deeper the more we go through
Learning and growing into more dimensional hues

Though many days may go by without verbalizing
How much you really do mean to me
Is genuine loving appreciation
To allow me to be all that I am
Without detouring my passionate path
That many times may even challenge you
Caressing unending supportiveness
You always stand by me
How can I really describe into words
All the love that we experience as it continues to grow
And all that you have been for me
I know you really do already know
Of the sparkle you have added to my life till now

All Encompassing Love

Love of the self is the greatest of all
flowing to everything inner and out
Seeing yourself in all that you experience
just knowing you are a part of all of divine innocence,
part of it all, just pure of love's grace

Stare at the blanket of soft grass
Imagine yourself lying on it, knowing its sharing with you
while the millions of strands tickle your flesh
As the radiant sun warms you into it relaxed feeling state
becoming trancified into everything you are intermingled with
a cosmic rhythmic dance of pure eternity

Hear the gentle waves as they brush against the sand
your body and mind are so serene you could stay here all day
You feel the warm breeze gently warming your skin
then you just realized you are imagining yet it felt so surreal

Though our body can be in one spot
The imaginative mind can create the most miraculous of stuff
When we become immersed through genuine focus
It will feel as real as we really did all that we imagined
This is our creative nature it has no boundaries to limit
Its only our own beliefs that alter it of our invisible permission
To take the plunge, be one with it all and let love soak it all up

AnnaMarie Antoski

Chapter 7

Travel

Bound

Traveling Roads

This chapter of traveling roads I wrote from my memories of some of the trips that I have taken. It has always amazed me how memories can be triggered upon so quick, most of the time, less then a split second in time. Just as we hear a song on the radio and within less then a fraction of a second it brings us back to the past of whatever we were doing when we heard the song. It could be many decades ago and still the memories comes into our perception so quick. Like a wisp of a thought brings the memory embedded in it and our senses all respond as if we were back in that time again.

It does leave me to wondering and pondering about the nature of reality, it does seem these memories we have preciously ingrained to bring up over and over again. Or is it we really revisit from the past experience that adds as it expands like an overlapping experience webbed through time and space. That we may not actually be retrieving, but reliving it in a revised created kind of way?

Just thought I'd leave you something to wonder about as we come to the end of my poetry book and the experiences we have shared. Though you were not literally with me, just by reading through the energy on these pages creates new experiences for you that you will also revisit in your future to your past. The indeed wondrous mystifying nature of reality.

These few poems are exactly like that, from the depth of my mind, revisited in an infinity of memories so intertwined, as I invoked the thought memory of the place I was at, I just wrote what surfaced and experienced all my senses to perceive as if I was there revisiting.

AnnaMarie Antoski

Elvis Spirit Lingers

As I am standing here, awesomely struck
Of a dream come true
In Memphis Tennessee
Strolling along Elvis's boulevard
In the dark hot summer's night
As I walk up to Elvis' mansion gate
The cement wall is filled with writing
From all who cherishes his memory

I am in such a trance
Just thinking of the King
His preciousness to this world
The energy snaps me back
Realizing that I have to wait
Till tomorrow to walk upon his land to his gate

As the morning is barely dawning
I walk through to the King's land
Still so awesome struck
As I can feel his Spirit all around

As we walk through every room
There's no doubt we all do feel and know
Elvis has not left this building
We can feel him everywhere

Or is it residue of His Great Energy
That eludes his magnetism or charisma
That will never die
It will infinitely linger here to roam

Smoky Mountains

What a destiny
Being in Tennessee
Strolling around the magnificent Hotel
With so much beauty all around
Though a challenge to leave
So much we have enjoyed and experienced to conceive
Our last part of the trip
Is to drive up the smoky mountains
Such magnificence for our vision to see

Long stretching hills
Just two lanes to go up or down
Higher and higher
Curve to curve
As we stop to view each scenic place
Nestled through the mountains
Peering into past memories
Of generations of people that lived in these hills
Now historic monuments
Of homes, churches, grave sites and schools

Awesome clouds lingering low
Felt like I could touch them
Deceived perception to behold
Streams flowing so peaceful and serene
As we each our packed lunch
While dangling our feet in the clean crisp flowing water

AnnaMarie Antoski

Darker it gets
As we drive farther up
Hundreds of fire flies glistening their shine
Some in bunches, yet others veer off
Spectacular show keeping us memorized for more

Our last night in Tennessee
As we sip on some red wine
Staring out the hotel window
Oh just so sublime
Set below of the smoky mountains we just ventured
Sparked of the lights shining bright on the streets
What tranquil visions to put us to sleep

Down in the Mine

We're on our way to Florida
Veered off our path to see the mine
It was worth the little detour
To experience what we hoped to find

Through the long hall tunnel
Light decreasing as we went
Then down an elevator
So far down we seem to go
Then the elevator stopped
The few of us got off

Into what seemed another world to me
Surrounded by rock, cement and machinery
Some tucked into the wall
Historical souvenirs relishing its past echoing that lasts
Interesting indeed to examine more closely for clues left in the residue

As I revel in silent focus connect in their time
Trying to pick up on all the timeless energies
Sparking of the miners memories that are imprinted
for this future for me to find

For a few moments my senses unravel
To hear rumbling of talking
and loud noises of machinery banging of its production
some leaving for breaks, or is my imagination running wild

An underground world
In the past was filled with miners doing their work
I try to imagine each day of all the hours
Not seeing the light of day that the mine devours

Majestic Florida

Such a heavenly place
Palm trees lining every street
Summery stores along the beach
filled with unique things
that fill the shelves as we seek

The seeming infinite road
that stretches in the oceans sand
traffic driving along
while we sit upon the sand observing all that we can

Hot breeze tickling our feet
Warm air penetrating our body
Caressing us with its relaxing potion of invisible lotion
So spectacular it does make me feel
Especially when knowing it's the middle of November
Yet back home the roads were filled with a blizzard of snow

My first taste of salty water
Shocking my taste buds of such a new experience
While the rolling deep waves streamed and pushed me along
Feeling a little delirious staring out at the oceans horizon
Quite the sensation caressed in Florida's Daytona Beach
Amazing as its been so many years
Yet the memories are so vivid
As if I am experiencing it right now
Tasting the salt on my tongue
As my mouth pouts it out

DISNEY LAND FUN

What a fantasy world
With so much to see and do
Taking us four days and yet not experiencing it all

Whirling roller coaster in the dark
Riding like Peter Pan
Up so close to the King Kong, almost touching it's hand
Wondrous indeed on the adventurous ride
Of It's a small world we ventured
Of cultures and song, so unified

Back to the future
I just couldn't get enough of
The kids kept on yelling
Come on mom, but I kept wanting one more ride

Simulations of exited exhilaration
As our seats moved back and forth
Twisting and turning our perception
Feeling so real, moving in motion
Of what was on the screen didn't mean a thing
We felt we were one with it all

Locked into a time warp
Of Ghost Buster reality
Watching Blue's Brothers car driving up and down
Overflowing fun of every step and every curve

The highlight of the night
As the magnificent sun dawned of its light
That allowed the radiant glow
Of a spectacular show
Of fireworks lighting the sky

A Little Bar

in

Nova Scotia

As we walk into the tiny bar
With friendly people filling the room
Takes us almost a half hour
To get to our seat
From talking to everyone along the way we'd meet

Feeling all like family
As if we have known them for an infinity
They're all so kind, making us feel so comfortable
In this Nova Scotia land that is so grand

As we sit waiting to be served
More people to meet
As they join us
And we talk
They share their lives and we share ours
Reminds me of what heaven would be like
No worries or cares
Just everyone helpful and sharing
Such genuine integrity

SPIRIT OF THE LIGHTHOUSE

I watch the lighthouse from a distant
As we travel up the winding road
Driving along the ocean's bank
Seashells everywhere to be found

Closer, closer we are now upon it
Up we go along the narrow stairway
That takes us up to the top

What a vision to perceive
I am so lost in a trance
Then next thing I know
I see a vision beside the wall
Radiating a white illuminating glow
Appearing like a sailor popping up to say hello

My mind fills with visions of exuberant data
Of a death at sea
While another waits for him
But he never does come home

I know imagination is wild
Yet I've learned that it's a dimension out of linear time
When we are deeply in focus
We can expand and pick up information
Of energy that vibrates of memories so vivid

The sailors emanating spirit that glowed
Now has disappeared into the lit wall
Leaving me with his story and memory
For me to further explore

AnnaMarie Antoski

OUT OF BODY, HERE I GO

Lying so relaxed, my mind is wandering
Stop it I do as I focus deeply, so intense so I can let go
Of everything except the release that allows myself to be so free
As I keep my focus on my body becoming so heavily
Feelings become tingling, I feel the sensation
Heavier yet lifting

My body seems so dense as the bigger part of me lifts
Like an enormous expanding unifying floating
As I keep my focus, if I don't I will slide back into body
I keep going with the serene paradoxical uncomfortable feeling
as I look down at my body
While the bigger spiritual real part of me
Floats above the house, above the clouds in the sky
Above into the brightness of it all as it heightens
Yet more clearly I can see, all that seems so unreal
Is more real than I ever felt,
Knowing this is the most rapturistic experience
As I look below as if I am in a hovering plane
Wanting only to go up, not down from once I came

As my thoughts focus back on my body
I feel a gentle release
Zooming in such a swish
Like a sped up zoom lens projecting me
Downward I go and in what seemed an instant I was back
In my body with new added memories that will create
My next out of body experience that I can track

Homeward

Of every trip I always wonder quite a bit
  When I am homeward bound
    That I miss all the people I have met from every town
      Of each place I go
        I have this deep feeling of how I just want to stay
          While simultaneously my heart is missing home
            Of all that are so dear to me

When I walk in the door
  Everything feels so different to me
    Like the room has somehow rearranged itself
      Quite differently then when I left

To realize these subtle changes
  So sensitive to my sensations
    How much a trip has changed me
      With everyone and everything I experienced

AnnaMarie Antoski

Chapter 8

Knowledge Transforms To Wisdom

Knowledge Transforms to Wisdom

Knowledge is power that's what is said
Though we can have all the knowledge absorbed in our heads
If we don't experience the knowledge in our own lives
We will be living an illusion to thrive

For knowledge to be in It's ultimate best
Is to take the knowledge to its magnificent test
By living it in our lives to have the experience
Then we will have transformed the knowledge
Into feeling and knowing
From what we have lived

Experience will always be the teacher for us
That transforms all knowledge to wisdom that we can then
trust
For when we have lived it
We have the proof to know
Then nothing can mislead us
We become the wisdom to own

MAGICAL

MIRACLES

MODERN DAY SPELLS ARE AFFIRMATIONS

In our past lives we were burned at the stake
But never oh never did we give up our estates
Of powerful mind and being that we are
Nothing could stop us to unfold to be known
Of the beings of magic
Our heritage we hold

In the past we used the tools of spells and incantations to do
The magic that we always had in our being that was our truth
As times changed we created to sustain to elude
Modern day affirmations instead
Much more accepted and no longer tossed into the wind
We are always stronger then whence we began

Our bewitching unfolds
Into our knowing to own
Into a reality that proves
We are more then what we appeared
Of Darrin's limits that always deceived
Of his rational conformity
Always trying to trick one's to believe
Instead we are like Samantha

Free to fly and do all we please
Because we never give up our sovereignty
That powers our natural being

Zap zap all possibilities become true
Just as twitching our noses
Or snapping our fingers
We can become more then once before
Blossoms of flowering
Our powers are intact
To be the craft that now never holds back

Expand and unfold into our destiny we call forth
Allowing the expansion to follow our own growth
Bewitched yet bewildered we may appear
We know our own kind
As we have thinned all the veils
To clearly be wise to never alter our divine
We broke Darrin down
He has now resigned
Without all these controls
We are so free we are the sovereign kind

AnnaMarie Antoski

I AM FOR I AM I AFFIRM IT TO BE

I am powerful … I am indeed
Don't just look at the external
Go beyond this illusion past just belief
Be the affirmation
Allow it to flow through
To see what is really powerfully true

All is just energy
Abbra Cadabra ohm so me ohm
There is magic for everyone to own

Stir the brew of thoughts to become
Of any desire that is risen to know
It will be revealed when relaxation is felt
Into a trance of the powerful gap
Where all is one
You can feel it
Like a click of a switch
Our mind just connects
Our power is united with the absolute infinite

The stillness of the void
The power is released
Everything is possible
When we know it… into wisdom we retreat

CHANGE THE THOUGHT TO MANIFEST IT OR NOT

So easily we could be deceived
If we don't beware of how linear time can cast the illusion
Like a hypnotic spell that can keep one stuck
When continuity appears so real
One only needs to go deeper into true reality

Where all is timeless and spacious
And we are continuously popping in and out
Mortal perceptions that are really delusional
When the immortal is always trying to peak out
Time is no thing when we learn to see beyond its construct
Then the hypnotic spell is broken
And the real truth is unveiled to know

Lickety split and it just is
All manifestations are manifested awaiting its physicality
When we drop the limited beliefs
We can choose a desire and have it manifested instantly
Only if we believed
But time slows down the process
Only because of the mortal thoughts
That dictates it to take time
Because it may be to spooky if not

Own it to know it then it will be created you will find
The owning is in the voided spaciousness
Where the infinite source does reside
Go there in purity the trust is unbendable
Walla will then become so instantly believable

AnnaMarie Antoski

THE HUMAN METAMORPHOUS OF CREATING

The biggest dreams that you desire
Are still lingering and have not transpired
You feel like giving up,
an hour goes by and you give it another thought
Is the testing time, not the end of the line
It's when your trust and faith is challenged once again

This is the stage where most let depression set in
When it really should be a celebration instead
It's surely the blossoming of thy seeds
To just let go, surrender it all, to allow it to be
But keep the knowing it may be closer then you ever did think

Remember the metamorphous that a caterpillar goes through
 Crawling around seeming so primitive
Struggles to get out of its cocoon but it never gives up
Pushing until it transforms into the butterfly
It flies away, new adventures comes its way

A chick that's in its egg stage
Pecks and pecks till it breaks out of its shell
Just as a new born babe
Comes from the mothers sac
It's so natural in nature, a part of each stage
From darkness into the light
As humans we do the same thing

In the darkness of not knowing we are creators creating
Till we come to know, we see the light
Of how we conceive to manifesting
All from what we believe

From an invisible realm of desired thought
The more focus and feeling we give it in our dark imaginative soil
It grows and grows till one day the desired cocoon
Sheds into light
As we let go in surrendering it becomes manifested in physical

Lingering Residue is but an Echo

Hark all my brethrens, there is so much to meet thy skies
Of things seemingly beyond mere comprehension
Enfolding dimensions with every thought disguised
Of infinite forever lingering intension
The terrified ego can get so scared
Inviting the natural self to do its transformations instead

Riding through the wildest stages of growth
And hanging on for dear life
To the eventual merging ego with the higher infinite self
Tapestry of the heavenliest experiences to be webbed
Released of any wondering seems to cease
All knowledge becomes for you to know
All questions become answered almost instantaneously as we grow

To know the beckoning reason
When we ask it is always given
The answer and the question are so miraculously combined
We find the lingering residue is but an infinite echo
Unified of illusionary parts of separation
Time and space blur into the echo of infinity
Then everything becomes to be realized

You begin to feel the aware creator
You begin to know the biggest reason for being
You begin to see all parts and pieces of their whole
Lingering its echo's in the holographic realm
That All That really Is, Is always there to know

Imagining to Manifesting

Let the morning sunrise caress you soul
   As the divine interwoven colors bestow upon your eyes to know
   As the warm breeze breathes upon your skin
   Allowing natures purity to awaken all your senses to rapture in
To a new day to create it to be
Just as you always dreamed is the secret key

   As the dew sprinkles upon your feet
   Letting you know all is so complete
   As bliss and harmony is everywhere to be found
   All it takes is just looking around
In the present moment of life
Where all is unfolding just right

   Letting the Creator flow through you
   As your journey into this physical life is renewed
   Can be anything you ever can imagine it to be
   There is no never really any impossibilities
Only truly imagining desires
Transformed from within your mind
to the external physical world you will find

   All that you desired and wish for
   Are just a few feeling thoughts away and no more
   To be impressed upon your mind
So that the brain can develop its neuron circuits so refined
Then it will be just as you imagined it would
Real to experience with all your senses as you knew you could

Hush, hush whenever doubt does surface
Pick those weeds by rethinking your desire already manifested
You will find that it won't take too long
For you to have all that you ever wanted
This is the way of the Creator's creations
Imagining and feeling it as if it's already manifested
And blessing it with the highest appreciation

Once your desire is peaked like a baked cake
So clear in your inner mind unaltered and so knowing and pure
Go ahead, you will just know
When its time to put the icing on the baked cake,
like your peaked desire
The icing is the surrendering just like letting go
To sit in expectation to receive, as you trust from your heart
Knowing with your excitement its so on its way
What you will notice is, you can have your cake and eat it too

We are Beings of Love

How feelings of love entice our senses
Igniting all the bliss and heavenliness
A burst from our hearts, empowering joy to its ultimate
Caressing us in all that is, seeing only beauty
Judgment is a non thing, when immersed in pure love

Feelings overwhelm of ecstasy
Captured in genuine acceptance
Allowing of everything, nothing else seems to matter
Sustained of the wonders so magically, sparkling moments
Of perfection so divine, of love's feelings wrapped in all we perceive

Love is the reminder of our natural heritage
Of how we could be if we only could see
All of life through filters of love
Perpetually to be in an infinite love's essence
Endowed in all of our senses

That is what real true freedom is
Knowing that we have that choice
To choose neither as bad or good
It is always and only will be just different
Our freedom lies between the negative & positive,
in the bliss of the paradox
Stripped of all judging, just because we choose
It can only be through experiences that it brings us to be
Beings of love that we were created originally

First we need to fall so deeply in love
Then become so angry that it turns into hate
Rattling us over, into totally giving up
In the notion that the negative energy gives us a sour taste
Then forgiveness comes so naturally,

it's a desperate end transforming us to begin
Into loves energy of forever the infinite whim

All of it to remind us that love is our natural state
 What we are made of, unleashed from the ego's slate
  Penetrated in the best of it all
   That is what love is, that is what we naturally are
 Beings of love

Unleashed from the controlling ego
 Allowed to just drench in the feelings of love
  Seeing all to just be.....beings of love.....is everyone's fantasy
  Is everyone's destiny......is everyone's true genuine eternal seeds
   Once flourished, one can never go back to the negativity of hell
    As the memory of heaven ruptures through, every single time
    Reminding us that heaven is only a thought away
Bliss is our natural state

When life is lived through genuine love
 Heaven is everyone abound
 Always there waiting to be found
  Only a memory away, a breath, a thought, an alteration of energy
   Transformed from any negative to a positive, transformed into
the paradox state of love

Releasing trance excited feelings
 That we can bare everything, nothings to hard
  That love feelings in everything
   Our bodies feel lifted, like an infinite orgasm reaction
    The reality of love heals every cell in our body
     It's just love, it is felt within and without
We become so high that nothing can bring us down
 When they say, heaven above and hell below
  The true meaning is heaven is what we feel, so high,
   that nothing can bring us down
    When we're in the wisp of love, being our true selves
We're just Beings of love as we glow our light through the dark

AnnaMarie Antoski

HEAVEN OR HELL

Heaven or Hell, oh what will it be
Now that I know it is all up to me
Ah but how we've been fooled into believing
All just happens having nothing to do with ourselves
Such an illusion that's been webbed over our eyes
That really it's up to us,
To choose to take things good or bad
or just take it all astride

Haven't we all at one time or another
Asked in bad times, why me, how could this be?
Always wondering,
detouring us from the genuine source
When the solution and reason is so much
more simpler of course
All things we can change to be
By how we choose to react so we can be free

It's simple when we just take a longer look
To know that by one simple choice,
perpetually we can do or undo
We can make our life a living laugher of heaven
or raging frown of hell forever after

Don't despair, nothing really is worth the care
To sit in anguish of anger or dislike
Joy and laughter is most important for our health
While giving the energy to all the other negative things
Is like being in heaven, enjoying laughter and fun
But instead moving into worrying
and disliking of things
Creating a hell of our daily hours,
Right in our own personal realities

Moving us surely from Heaven into Hell
or Hell into Heaven
When everything is really up to me and you
    Always a choice in our making, aware or unaware
        We are traveling in and out of it all of the time,
            we just have to beware

Negative or positive, an instantaneous switch,
    like a flick of a dime
        or a switch of a light, can turn darkness into light
        A smile into a frown, a laugh into a fear,
            or happiness into sadness
                Oh yes its all that near

They say that the fine line between all duals
    That travel like a two lane road
        Just with the drawing of a painted line will move all
            traffic to merge into one
                Just like we can be in anger one moment,
                    then hear something
                        funny and merge into laugher,
                            we then shine like the sun

The dogmas of religion want us to believe
    there are such places
        One up above...
            the other below but not right here or right now
                When in realities truth, it's right here on our earth
                    Not only a future place
                        to go to when we pass on from this Earth

Our challenge is so of this physical world we know
    To know heaven and hell
        and choose as the creator intended us to know
            Knowing it here in this planet of duplicity and duality
                To unite the paradox of confusing conformity's ways
                    To know that Heaven and Hell
                        is just a CHOICE away
                            That we live upon every minute of every day

Just by how we perceive whatever it is that's going on
Is the exact way we experience heaven or hell
I am now realizing how simple it really IS
And how it is so truly up to us, believe it or not,
   you know once you wake up

To sit in despair, worrying or dislike
Is like switching off the light
Is the same as enjoying Heaven or worrying of Hell
The good or the bad, the anger or the joy,
the laughter or the sad
   The judgments or the allowing,
   the expecting or accepting
    Is really is up to Us

And with energy being a factual proof
We add to mass's reality without a doubt, it so true
To help this planet become heaven or hell
To add to the heavenliness of heaven or the
hateful bloodshed of hell
   To shed tears of joy is exercise to employ
   But to shed tears of hatred of hellish ways,
   is to fight till life
    just a battling ground destroyed

We can live in Hell of the negative choice
or instead live in Heaven of laughter & joy
To be in Peace is to let go of all
expectations & seriousness
   Again we should ask,
   what is so important
    to take away our experiences of Heaven away

Do we want to choose hell or heaven
Fear or Love, it's all up to us,
   And so simple ... just a chosen thought a-way
   That simple process makes all the difference today

Any Negative Choose the Opposite of Love

Instead of problem choose opportunity
Instead of victim choose empowerment
Instead of hate choose love
Instead of lack choose unlimited
Instead of illness choose health
Instead of not liking choose accepting
When everything look so dark and bleak
Choose something to appreciate

Instead of complaining choose to imagine what you prefer
Instead of being depressed
choose the thoughts that make you feel so good
Instead of sadness choose always knowing there is more
That consciously you might not be aware of but
your larger source knows it all

Instead of disagreement choose it's only another way
Instead of judging choose differences
And feel the heaviness start to fade

Instead of can't choose yes I can
Instead of impossible choose to know all is possible
Because if you can think it then it already exists
From the infinite web of consciousness that does persist

Instead of this is the way I am, choose I can always change
Instead of enemy see the love that's deeply hidden inside
Instead of dread choose hope
It's just a few vibrational frequencies off

Instead of doubt choose to believe
Instead of conforming choose to be unique
Instead of accidental choose its all creation
Instead of giving up choose to keep on going

Because your desire manifested
could just be around the next corner

Instead of blame choose to be responsible
for your creations
  Instead of the conformed way of pointing your finger
  Realize that it's just another learning opportunity
  Instead of incomplete choose to think and
  feel from the end
    Of how it can really be by focusing your attention
    As if it already is in your hand

Instead of reacting choose to respond
  Knowing reaction is automatic but to
    respond gives you time to ponder upon
      Choosing respons-i-bility,
        as it's the knowing of the ability
          that you always have the power,
            it's your divine fertility

Instead of being grateful choose to appreciate
Just because it's a higher vibration,
  never needed to negotiate
    Instead of being angry choose to be empathetic
    Instead of fear choose courage to walk you through
    Instead of pity choose sympathy
      it will lead you to empathy
        Instead of limited choose unlimited
          Instead of it's just another day
            choose it's my choice of how it unfolds my way

Instead of just reading this … make it your daily mantra
  The more you do something repetitiously
    the more you are reprogramming your plan
      Until you see your reflection in everything finally change
        Then you know that you are surely on your way
          to life becoming everything you want of your command

Instead of seeing everything and everyone separate
 choose to see through to the invisible where it's all unified
  See the connection to invisible to visible
   That's seeing through all illusion
    Knowing they are old past data of conclusions
     Reap the new ways that will transform your days

Instead of perceiving yourself as only physical
 Choose to see the bigger invisible part of you
  That can construct you to become renewed
   Instead of believing everything just happens to you
    Choose to know that you create every part

Instead of believing there is only one dimension
 Choose to perceive the infinite web
  In knowing you are part of it all instead
   See the light in all darkness to be revealed
    That love is the brightest embedded and sealed
     But if you don't you are still always loved
      Because the Source of Creation will never judge

Through this process you will experience divine esteem
 And a heavenly blissful life will gleam
  Where magic is not a fictional thing
   Instead it becomes your reality
    Your life transforms to reflect it all
     Because you choose to turn everything to love
      Which is your natural infinite being
       Charisma and magnetism will be your rays
        Shining the light in the darkest days
         You will become the divine beam of love
          To be your divine blueprint of
           Just knowing you were always pure Love

Obsessed with Desire

Ah that knowing feeling of your desire so wanted
You become so obsessed with it that nothing else matters
Only the impressing it upon your brain/body, soul and heart
You just can't stop until you get what you want

That is how to deliberately manifest
When it becomes all you care to think about
Your desire, you want it, you just have to have it
Nothing will stop you until you get it

You will find that so naturally your thought become divine
Crowned with emotion and thought and felt
Such excitement pulsates within you
The vision become so clear and you see it everywhere

You finally get to the point you just have to let go
You have given it all you've could and even more
The release comes with a divine absolute knowing
Then it just pops into your physical reality
Before you realize your obsessive desire
has become your manifested reality

The Creator Put Everything We Need Inside

What is orgasm but to show us how to create
Bringing our desires to the magnificent peak
Fondling it with our imagination so specific
Until any thought of it is so pure in our vision

Then just as we go through our lovemaking
Enjoying every step of the way
Our desire is so pure that it's time for its pure releasing
Surrendering of letting go with trust, it's on its way

And enjoy the imagined desired manifested vision
Through the pulsation of your body's electrical currents
To physically feel from your inner imagination
It's the orgasm of desire manifested as the orgasm release
Ah into physical, feel its sensational experience manifested

Oh how alive you now feel that you are
Creator as the creator always desired you to
To know the creator built everything we could ever need
Into our own body for its imagining and release

Like a sign of a cross
Using your head for imagining and brain hardwiring
With the lowest chakra of your physical stimulant
Then to the left to merge the ego with the right soul
Merge it all together with the heart feeling
Then Walla, your desire is manifested

AnnaMarie Antoski

Pure and Whole the Gods We Are

You are a piece of the whole
  You shine like a radiant star
    Because you shine so bright
      Created from reality in your unique way

Irrelevant of where you are in space and time
  You are magnificent just because you are you
    Regardless of your stage of growth
      It's because unity is our oath

United we fell and united we grow
  Unified together we are the whole
    Fragments appearing separate
      Under the microscope of seeming individuals
        We are all pieces of the whole
          Everything affects everything we've come to know

Love in the most genuine sense is the root
  Judgment disappear in every reflection
    All those needs are disappearing
      Only cravings of the now is what we want
        Life becomes a daily joy
          Knowing it is always just up to us
            We celebrate the greatest celebration,
              the knowing we are the gods

Adult Fairy Tales

We began our lives with many fairy tales
Santa, the tooth fairy, peter pan, witches, Jack and the bean stalk
Last but not least, that everything just happens to us
All these tales that gave the child a magical feeling towards life
Then disillusion the child with adult truth
Crumbling the child to become saddened with the shock
Of magic just disappearing into a hardened survival world thus of

Years of adolescence that many rebelled
Trying to keep soul dignity of their self esteem
Punished consistently for having their own truths
Pushing until they conform to the norm
Leaving all magic and god esteem in the past
Into a life of struggle and worry, with little good feelings left
The adult fairy tale that grew into mass reality
Of beliefs that smothered our natural selves, removed from Creation

Until one day we stumble upon
Information, knowledge that resonates with our heart
Feeling so good, making so much sense
We ponder and delve into it with such curiosity and wonder
The knowledge gives us such a soft warm feeling of empowerment

Magically blending our lives back into us having control
Where wishes, prayer, meditation, spells all seem to work
We realize we went from child like fairy tales into adult myth tales
And finally broke through to an enlightened powerful state
A place from within of a resonate knowing

That reality's created from repetitious thoughts
Flavored with emotions into feeling
Basking in imagination as if it was
How wisdom is so like that, leaving us to our own responsibility
Giving thanks for the truth to be known
That life is as magical as we allow it to be perceived

GOD AWAKENING

Free oh how free
This feeling and knowing is for me
I have no more cares
Because I am in the arms of the ultimate best
Of all power and radiance
The dance is so divine
Lifting me higher then I ever been in this time

Basking in the knowing
It's all up to me
Stay consciously connected
Everything then is at my command
All power available to create all that I can
Living the life I had only dreams about
Just like magic, fades away all doubt

Free we all can be
When we feel it from within thee
Activate the God gene
Then just enjoy the manifested beam
You'll go higher into the infinite ride
Into a feeling of blissful tides

Nothing else matters
Only this feeling that's inside
Expanding like a fountain of love
Caressing every part
Power keeps increasing
Electrified in goose bumps to thy skin
Echoing of the God in us awakening

Reminiscing

In my haven, my heavenly space, months turn into years
Time passed through this space, so quickly
For me it was all sparks of eternity
I stayed forever so out of time
It was heavenly bliss I always desired to find

Many seasons sure did pass
Cold snowy days turned to nights
Winds shaking even my chair
I watched, I felt, I've been it all
All my past of my experiences

And my years of desired seclusion
To find myself, to find heaven
To know the wisdom, as all masters come to know

Merged in the sunrise and sunsets
I felt the hearts of the birds
The smiles of the bunnies
The feelings of the hungry wolves
Life feeding on life
Wondering when enough would be enough

I watched the bright sky turn so dark
Till all the stars shone, twinkling their brilliant light
And silence was crisp as the white pure falling snow
When my frozen fingers almost felt good
Peace enticed me making me feel so neutral
Feeling so a part of everything I seen
A neutral bliss that was steadfast and expanding into forever

IT'S ALL ABOUT FUN

Guidance, direction
Oh which way to go
When feeling confuses
Choose what feels good
As your compass to know

Fun, if its fun
You're on the right track
Oh yes, fun, is really where it's at
Turn it to joy
feel the excitement begin

If life's not the way you want it
And you say it's not your fault
Dear one it's all really up to you
Always your choice
You just were not aware
Up until now
You know deep inside
It's the only way to go

LINEAR DECEPTIONS

What a splendid time we are living
To know so much more then before
More collective consciousness realizing
As it gathers more momentum

As we look up to our skies
In the darken night that allows our vision to behold
All the shining things that seem invisible in the daylight
As there is no contrast that allows us to see what is always there
But is invisible to perceive because of our beliefs
We need the darken sky's background
So what's invisible can be visible

We are looking at our past
As the sparkling stars that have already exploded
Hundreds and thousands of years ago
Yet they seem still so real to our perception
As if we are viewing beauty of its presence

How can that be that we are seeing above into our past
As we live to perceive our linear lunacy
Of so many illusions that seem of true fact

How slowed down is the physical reality we call earth
When we are seeing the stars past
So much ought to be considered if genuine truth is enable to lurk

It's like sitting in a movie theatre
Watching a movie that is projected on a screen
We know the real actors are not presently performing
They have created the film months or years ago to be seen
Captured onto a recording to be viewed at a later date
For the actors it's their future

Yet for us it's our present
Just as the stars in the sky can shine rays of its wisdom

For us viewing the recording it's then the actors past
Yet in our present we watch and evoke emotions
Of something that is left up to our own perceptions
Just for the experience of entertainment to enjoy

Is just as the night skies is our film of time
Projected from our own minds
Conformed through what we were taught to believe
Projected outwardly to be deceived
Through our linear perception is surely a deception

So we are only looking at a film memory of yesterdays
And making it appear as if it's today
Evoking such emotional stimulant
That becomes funneled into feelings through our hearts
And we bask in the magnificence
Of a past we continually keep revisiting

Anything we feel and experience from our Sun
Takes 8 minutes to reach us in physical
Again we experience a blast from the past
Because we are fooled again by our linear deception so fast

That is how powerful we really are
We even deceive our own selves of what's really going on
Denying knowledge to continue to live in illusions
For the pleasure of beliefs that keep us pretending
Until the wise rises in us to know
Everything is much more then linear deception pretends it to be
So evolving when we allow it to be our destiny,
 to know what there is to know

Creating by Feelings...

If you want it, you can have it
　All you have to do is feel it
　　Feel as if you already are
　　　And it will become
　　　　Created for you to experience

If you think from automatic habit
　You will miss all magnificent that is there to feel
　　Just by flipping to the other side
　　　Where bliss and heaven await
　　　　Just by feeling puts your thoughts in motion

Don't cha know it's always been this way
　Only difference you were not aware
　　You've been creating everything
　　　Just by focusing into feel
　　　　Creating life in feeling momentum

Those goose bump feelings
　Are creating memories
　　Whatever you get you created
　　　Just to know it is the greatest blessing
　　　　That is always was and is up to you

AnnaMarie Antoski

Invisible to Visible

Born into physical bodies from the invisible dimension
All solid objects manifested from the
  invisible thoughts of desires
Emotions of felt feelings from invisible beliefs triggered
An appearing solid unit, our physical body consisting
  from trillions of inner cells
    Everything appearing separate,
      yet is united from one source of it all

A cell or cordless phone from invisible frequency signals
Hundreds of visual channeled programs
  from invisible signals of energy vibrations
  All we see, feel, taste, smell and hear,
    all from invisible inner signals that go so unnoticed
Continuous motion of our reality is from
  invisible frozen bits of snapshots of memories
    Just like a video recording is spliced and edited
      together from frames previously taken
        then viewed in a future time
          all perceptions of illusion making it seem real

As a clock ticks away
  For one it can go by so slow
    when they dread what they do
    For another it can go by so fast from loving it instead
    Yet it's still all just experiences
      Loss or gain is dependant from the one
        who is experiencing

An infinite dimension more real then in physical
  Yet perceived as physical death of passing on
    Resulted from beliefs valued to extremes
      Invisible to physical perpetually it goes on to deceive

It's Always a Return to Source's Love

Just as I think I made so much progress
Releasing judgments and expanding my consciousness
More residues enfolds for my observance
To challenge me with opportunities to realize
When I thought I was so close, really I am so far
It is becoming more natural now to respond differently
From years of practice it's becoming habitual with dignity
Once anger and hate of others triggered me
Of how they are not I intend them to be
Now becomes for me to reflect what I need to learn to progress
So exuberant is this returning to Source's Love

As it has been said by many masters
If it's inside, then it will surely be triggered to be shown
My free will of transforming my reactions of fear and denial
To responses of growth and reflection to evolve
Has allowed me to be at peace in my expanding eternal growth
I now can give thanks for all that I realize
It's in those opportunities that I grow the most now with loving intent
When in the past when anger would reign
I now take hold to see my truth
That all does return to Source's love is to be known

Now more and more of my reactions are responses
Eased of any resistance
It surely is truth, when we just grow to know Source
Since that it where the flow extends
Just like a freshly planted tree
The challenges perpetually strengthen me
To take root of the Divine Loving Sources soil
Intertwined in all the loving ways
Since everything that I put out
Returns to me without a doubt
No longer do I need to waste my energy when all my ego's fears have
returned to Source's love

AnnaMarie Antoski

When Forgiveness Becomes Genuine

Forgiving seemed easy to me
I've done it thousands of times with almost everything
and others including me
Till I became stuck after forgiving all through my life
Like a final straw that just persisted creating so much resistance
For me to forgive from my loving heart

I worked on it daily that is what I thought
Yet what was coming out was not love it was still fear
extended with anger
Keeping me stuck without my realization
Then I compared my feelings of what I felt to real love
Quite the opposition that even tricked me
When I thought I had it all worked out

Now I clearly see what I had hidden harboring inside me
Still lots of residue of the altered ego that took me over
And kept me there for longer then I even knew
Till now, like a shining knowing that always works
To show us the light through the darkness
that can keep us stuck
I felt at peace, to feel the differences
that is now setting me free
Where I really want to be

Knowing true love needs no apologize
It's unconditionally just accepting
Just allowing others journeys to travel
When they rumble my divinity
Then I still have left over residue
So I return to my learning in progress
To learn and grow from where I became stuck
Released now of resistance and just free flowing
Where all love is always at
And how does that feel, just magnificent
I kept my distance to know myself
Of what was left inside, that had to be triggered out
In maybe my last ego's reluctance
To finally unite with my natural god self
No longer to need to alter my bliss
Viewing it now from love's roots
The only source that feels the best
And will always lead me in the direction
of my god self to caress

ATTITUDE

IS

EVERYTHING

In everything and of everyone
Whatever appears to be and show doom or gloom
or heavenliness
It's all in your own creation
Wrapped up in attitude

Irrelevant of any situation or any interaction
You thought the thought and give it energy to grow
No use complaining, when it's all up to you
Take your power back, and choose what to think
Make your attitude sparkle and watch it glow

Before you know it
You'll be seeing what you truly want
It's all up to you and the sooner you know
You have always been the one in control

Judgment Removed

In the twilight of the night when everything seems so quiet and right
In the past I used to worry about the birds and how they survived
Such cold bitter winds and snow
And all the other animals that also roam
How do they all survive all of these storms

Now I realize how I perceive came from what I believed
If I perceive everything as a victim with negative consequence
That was a perception coming from me
From what I believed and all life to be
Like ah the poor things that needed to be saved
As I believed I needed to be saved
With no trust in my own self

Then I learned the essentials of energy
And of a Source I once perceived as God
All we think becomes beliefs and our reality
A seemingly simple thing as a belief in victimhood
Created everything in my life to be of that alignment and experience
Perception makes all the difference in what we do observe
And how we actually observe it
Will create what we literally perceive

With that changing shifting of mindset
I became to see it was true
I didn't need to be saved I only needed just to know
Knowledge of who I really was and created from
That knowledge shifted all my perceptions
Leaving me so free

I see that Source of All That Is supplying everything
The birds always survive and never judge
A newly planted tree cannot connect it roots firmly in the ground
Without the winds and storms that
        strengthen them to become strong
Just as the cocoon needs the struggle
                to become a free butterfly

That it was me judging everything through victims sighs
Now that I know even that all and everything is taken care of
Just by connecting to the Infinite Source of All That Is
I no longer perceive victimhood to alter my peace
Where everything is taken care of if we shift our beliefs

Into that knowing melts all doubts and fears away
Now I see the beauty of everything and the ease of the flow
Without judging anything it truly becomes heaven on earth
Without worry the beauty of Source's patterns unfold
Without fear there is only Sources extended eternal trust
With out the perceptional beliefs in lack
We then see the eternal abundance of it all
Without our focus on fear
Real love is in everyone and in all things
There then is only blissful peace of enjoying
  everything I bestow

Our body's natural state is to heal if it's disharmonized
That is the way our bodies were designed
It's only our doubting beliefs that alter its performance
Once we know that all is already taken care of that way
We need to do nothing but love it
  and allow the sources eternal flow

We don't need to be saved
We just need to be and allow our natural state to flow
Then behold there no longer would be any disease
Dysfunctioning us from our nature ease

We are creators creating every single bit of our realities
To connect all the dots to see that truth
One has to observe long enough to see all the proof
Then all beliefs surely dissolve
  into the absolute pure knowing
One looks no further then to themselves to keep growing
As that is where the connection really is
Inward to our natural selves that is directly linked to Infinite Source

Basking

in Our

Infinite Self

Words cannot describe the connection to our infinite self
It's allowing our heart to filled with love to be felt
Of emotional connects from our inner being
Unfolding into all we are perceiving
It truly is only a little web,
showing us
Paradise, heavenliness,
eternal love of ecstasy and bliss

The state of being is so expanding and alive
with a magnificent momentum of omnipotence
All in the powerful now to reside
Revelation feelings of peaceful essence
Released of any resistance, doubt, polarity or judgments
It's a united and unified, totality of what we truly are

Our spiritual self merged into our physical
Totally connected of the Source of all infinite
Expands into everything we then feel and experience
Like an infinite focus that expands forever
from the momentum of now together
Of a highest vibration of freedom to be our natural self
Everything collapses into whole, health,
youth, abundance
In constant flow now of a heartfelt desire

Now eternally motivated to never expire
that brought us to that knowing of experience
And it continuously flows
Feeling light as a cloud
Shining bright as a star
Warming everything in our path like a brilliant star

Creating galaxies and universes from our feeling thought
Seeding and growing eternally forever to be sought
So naturally, so in flow,
so harmonious of the highest vibration we go
of our truest nature
It is the highest joy and freedom,
heavenly bliss of all possibilities
Knowing we are connected to our infinite self

The Trick of the Ego

Just when I really thought I had it so in control
I should have realized because I could feel myself becoming
less then I know
In the words I was using,
which I know words are an end result
Of beliefs we value even if it is not what we want

For years I did see the teeter tottering back and forth
When my ego was so strong
and just did not want to let go
Then I realized that I bought into my ego symptoms
that I allowed to possess me
Though it only took the momentum of recognition
The habitual patterns were so strong and kept hanging in

Though in that knowing that I can recreate all new beliefs
To actually transform to know
instead of stay in denial of my ignorance
I did the Love work that allowed me to grow
Into absolutely knowing it was my altered ego
still taking me over

And though it was becoming less everyday
Some days though very few in comparison
to the past that I knew
Showed me some left over residue that just was so stubborn to let go
And though my dear you took the repercussion
And though we both know that real love

is never to be sorry
Because it is rooted in total unconditional to not sway

All now I can say, this is a new day
And from the comparison from dark into light
And in the dark whence sometimes I fall
And pick on you in devious ways
It really didn't feel good for me or for you, I do know
And of course that is the perfect sign
to know the ego must go
Gently and lovingly I tell it no more
Be at peace allow itself to unite
and become so much more
As that what will be with every merging piece
Of left over residue
That alters my peace of bliss
That also affects all and everything around me
This always is the return to real love

Reflections Hold Many Secrets

Many things we say and do
Many still do not want to hold the mirror
To reflect if I see it in you
Then it must be in me too
The more I expand in source's love I surely do feel
The things that used to irritate me
are now like ice cubes melting away

Though you may appear as an enemy one I used to hate
You were the best teacher challenging every single thing
From every one of the challenges I could have run away
But I surely did know
That I would have found others
who would do the same work
So I did use you as an opportunity for me to surely grow
And in that growth I did find
All that I resisted in you was what was in me too

It's a brave one who can see this so clearly
To use every challenge as a absolute opportunity
To allow our higher natural selves to come through
Perpetually until we are refined
Into a being of love
That eventually never holds conditions
It knows of no such thing
Because it is what we once left in eternity

The more I resisted the more work I knew I had to do
Now eventually through the years
I have become all I have wanted to become
Though I hold no recognition in society's standards
Divine has no standards
Just the rewards of total love that transform everything in its path
The reward of heavenly bliss and no more alterations that last
Altered ego finally unites, with its desire to be one of the whole
The ecstasy feelings are too great
And is when falling has no more attraction
We know we have final arrived

THE BLISSFUL VIBE

I'm on a blissful vibe
Oh such a heavenly ride
I took all my power back
And own myself, I'll never look back

Oh such a blissful vibe
Magical empowering ride
Staying in the now is where all the power is
Where everything is possible just from belief

Nothing else matters
Only what you desire
And be it, feel it,
in that knowing are creating it

We're on a blissful vibe
Oh such a heavenly ride
Where thoughts do create reality
When fueled with intense feeling you will just be
The I am that that I am

Come on the blissful vibe
Have such a heavenly ride
Then your will see
It's all true to be
Know, knowing is creating reality
Know, now is the powerful state
Just from that all will expand
Be it, know it, feel it with all your heart
And bliss will be the ride of your life

2012 A Journey to Evolve in Joy

Don't let them scare you
To create so much fear
The dooming is not upon us
It is now so clear
Predictions of the past were only warnings to get our attention
We got it, we owned it, and changed it to never threaten us again

All it took was a collective few
When we compare it to billions on earth
Just one percent to do the great work
Was all it took to change our doomed destiny
We are free from all that held us prisoners
In our realities that appeared so out of control
We took our power back now we're arriving at last
To a new world, new earth, new heavenly plane

Just in all our lives
Every all our challenges are just a mask for our blessed opportunities
To dissolve the mask and shine our light to grow into excelled
ecstasy
The courageous ones that found the truth and expanded for the rest
to follow to
We surely did, create the platform to build heaven on earth
The residues of chaotic waves are just passing through
Like a mother giving birth
Of course there is some pain in delivering the new babe
Just as our earth is grown and the birthing pains
Are lingering from all the old energies
Its laboring is coming to pass
And the babe of a new earth, new ways, new lives to live
Is seen just as that a few final pats on the back

To deliver all our souls have waited for

Just a few from a billion to collectively energize
The miraculous world that we will all surely enjoy
Just what our purposeful journeys were for
Paradise to find all expanded from our intentions
Energizes with such perfections
Is our future created from eternally now
We give great forever thanks
That we found our divine place from our higher soul's selves
United with our physical and now we rejoice
Not ever having to move in linear one pace
Its was all from the internal to expand into external
We knew it and did it, just like creative gods do

Whole and Owning It

In awake meditation, just being in the now
Eternally expanding in the blissful joy all around
The darkness of the night and silence of all sound
As hundreds of acres of land surrounds
Not a peep from the forest
Only the silent exuding stars in the dark sky
For hours I just sit in the joy of observance of all that is felt

As the expanding now of eternity
Allows the day to unfold
I experience the oneness of it all
As I now hear the chirping of the birds
Magnificent symphony of a multitude of different chirps
The most divine beauty to my ears
Nature awakening joyfully in harmony
As the darken sky is also unfolding
Its most exuberant colors in the horizons
Feels like watching heaven awakening to its
early dawn

Describing it in physical words surely
is only fractional
As it's in the feeling that can only be felt
As my heart expands with such delight
Of such grateful appreciation
to experience this in physical
Embodied in my senses of the most magnificence
of the infinite
Peeking and showing itself to me
As if to express its oneness in its reflection back to me
Of being a part of it all just so naturally

Brighter and brighter it perpetually becomes
Bird's expressions of they're naturalness to it all
Colors are so brilliant and mixed of their prisms
In a giant holographic passion
expressed in physical
Beauty of it breathing into my soul
In the appreciation that I am also
a part of it all...

Chaos to New Structures
of Heaven on Earth

Life in the now expanding so powerfully
Collective consciousness is catching up
All old structures are falling apart
Creating the space for the new energy state
To expand in its cultivation

More and more individuals are realizing
The creators they are and are creating deliberately
Allowing their connection to all that is
Becoming the power we always had within
Lifted in joy, feelings of heavenly bliss

Heaven on earth is becoming expanded
From the small few who have expressed
Then many divine intuitions has followed
More and more are becoming in light of
Perpetually expanding heaven consciousness

Daily, minutely creating our new earth
Of empowerment and bliss
Creating the grounding
Old structures collapsing chaotically destructing
Paving the new structure of powerful bliss in the old space

AnnaMarie Antoski

MIRROR

MIRROR WHAT DO I SEE

Blame complain is that what many do
Judge, curse everyone who is not what they want
Condemn, control, then its time to let go
Source only gives without any judging to consider

Source knows no conditions
Just gives what you put out
If you speak and feel about it
That's what you get back
It has no conditions it only knows real love
So whatever you are getting is what you put out

All reflection is from only you
Just like a mirror showing you back to you
The only change that makes any difference
Is the changing of one own self
Then the reflection will mirror it out

Mirror mirror is not only on the wall
It is reflected in everything you perceive in all
You are a living mirror and only see what you believe
What you put out in thinking and feelings
Is exactly what will reflect back
The mirror will never deceive

To know this true is the absolute freedom and peace
We all desire it is within
When we see through the fog
Through the clarity of it All

ILLUSION OF THE WORLD

Most of the world is afraid
Let them tell you what they will
They don't know,
 they're all going on their own ego's
enslaved to whatever is programmed to do
when no one tells you all the truth

It's in vein, all in the human game
keeping us as slaves
get insurance, paying out high demands
then when it comes to use it
they say oh sorry we just can't

Programmed us to believe
that is what we need
you must be insured, cause what if something happens
Hmm I am not so sure
because paying for something that has not happened
is a sure way to create it to be
paying in advance for a future reality

Life, death, vehicle, health,
everyone is insures to the hilts
yet then having no money left
it's all going out to future of what never became
unless we focus on it enough then we create it
as it sits in illusion seeming so sane
Locked into the fears of the world and feeling so lame

When is it time to say no
No to all that enslaves
To all the insurances that we all are programmed to pay
for a future that they programmed us to believe
The what ifs that may happen
You better be safe then sorry
When it's all made to deceive

We are creating our future
By what we believe
What we think about now, not one minute in advance
For a life that I am creating
There is no room for being so unconscious
Freedom is what fear deceivers will strip you of
all love's divinity
I am taking my power back
So I can finally be free

Giving and Receiving

Giving and Receiving are the same energy
 As the creator gives and receives our experiences
  We're in an Infinite Hologram
   All pieces of the whole of an Infinite One

What we see is what we get
 What we give is what we get back
  It multiplies in multi-folds
   Because it's a high vibration
    Especially when we give because we want to
     That is giving from the Heart

Whatever we see in another
 Is only a reflection back
  A mirror of our own perception
   An opportunity to expand our growth
    In releasing all judgments
     In creating our life heavenly

To give is to receive
 It's a boomerang effect
  A little or a lot
   Doesn't matter when it's from the heart
    When we live life as a mirror
     We can only become refined and whole

Our heart is either overflowing with love
 Or restricted of its flow
  Sharing is giving and receiving
   Giving attracts receiving
    There is no blockage there
     It is all one energy
      Bubbling up of unified sharing
       Creating our lives in ecstasy
        When we respond lovingly
         Will be what will return to thee

SHINE

You gotta to know if you want to glow
You gotta to feel what you want to be
You gotta to think the higher vibe thoughts
That will create your reality to be what you want

Come on its way past time
This victimhood that's an old outdated song
Put some creator self esteem into your life
By owning yourself in every day in every way

What you believe is what you get
Being the slave to old stalemate beliefs
See the power when you let them go
And restructure powerful thoughts to guide you for more

The power is within when you let go of negative
Feel the upliftment every time you will shine
To feel the difference from your own heart
By responding differently then the old ways that kept you stuck

Shine to love yourself
Shine to own your creator you are
Shine to radiate the power of love
Shine your light of love thoughts
Be aware of what you are putting out
Cause that is exactly what you will get back
So shine your best on everything
You'll find heaven and the truest love
And it was all really within

HEREDITY IS UP TO YOU

Brown eyes, blue eyes, how about green
Thin hair, thick hair,
or no hair at all or a little in between
Young skin, old skin, health or disease
Natural hair color growing in
Or gray all from belief

The truth is out,
science now knows
Our DNA is programmed
all from our beliefs
If you think it
You sure do own it
And is what is creating you to be

Fat or slim, short or tall
Pessimistic or optimistic
Nothing is heredity at all
The truth is unveiled, we are set free
To create our bodies in
anyway we please

Perfect eye sigh, energy unlimited
Live the life, it's so permitted
Have your body only of your choice

Just pick new beliefs and feel it, see it as if it was
Your body cells will respond
And create it the way you want
Yes it's up to you, the creator you are
Just keep loving it into being

We create the programs, and our bodies respond
So you can create anything you want
Yes I'll say it again, it's totally up to you
Your body is your servant,
your beliefs create the program
Not heredity as once we once that we knew

173

Victim or Master ... It's all up to You

Are you living the life as a slave
Feeling like a victim and can't escape
Believing in the lies nothings really is up to you
Things just happen you think you are stuck forever
Then it surely is time to let go of those old thoughts

Its time now to make the shift
Shift into knowing why you exist
Take each experience and feel how it does
If you don't like it then switch to a new feeling that does

If you are sick, it's because you're thinking sick thoughts
If you look older you just stressed yourself out
If you still need addictions to fill your empty void
Then you are a victim like a slave desiring to break free

Take those old beliefs and trash them out
Think the new thoughts that will replace the old
Feel what its like to be like a god
Powerful and unlimited to have and be everything you want

Beliefs give the messages to the DNA
 into the genes to create
The chromosomes are eavesdropping
 on your every thought
 creating the beliefs just of what you know
know it, you own it, it is the way it always is and was
do you want to stay a slave or be a master
 it is all what you think
when you think it long enough it becomes a belief
then everything beckons at your command
your body your life all energy it attracts

Wake up the new you

Wake up, wake up, its time to know
You say you got problems
Well that's what you keep believing to own
Problems have the greatest gifts
When you be open to it you will know

Get out of self pity
And perceive everything as opportunity
You will grow, you will become to know
That all problems were just a step
To bring you to change your attitude

It's all up to you
Once you know it you will see
Everything can become so easily
It's really simple when you believe it is

Say it, sing it, tell yourself until you get it
It's all up to our own selves
To be the change we desire
See it feel it inside first
Then it will become just from thinking new way
You have the power
Its time to use it
For we are evolving to so much more

AnnaMarie Antoski

MY EGO SCREAMS

Oh how my ego fools me all the time
Get angry, be mad, ya its okay to feel that hate
Feel the evil bubbling up inside
Wanted to leash out at whatever comes my way
Be aggressive stand up for your rights
You are right, they are wrong
Just judge with all your might

My ego screams and I seem to obey
Till I opened myself to another new way
Calling on spirits of love to guide me through
Enough is enough, no more hate I want love
No more drowning till I can't get up
Love gently floats me high and above
Allowing me to see it's always my choice
To choose the fool of the ego or the love of my soul

Then comes the guilt, the killer of life
Why did I do that, I should have not reacted like that
Oh how my ego screams for me to do what I do
Then all of a sudden that old depression comes through
Down and out and hating myself
Taking another unconscious ride on my ego's self
Believing its right, I'm entitled, when it just feels so wrong

It was me all the time I was reflecting out
All the hateful vengeance of my own mirror
Peace took me over and now without a doubt
I feel the rising of love as it absorbed my ego
Oh such freedom I feel as my ego's released
No more hate and guilt for me to be enslaved
Love has conquered and I am free
All I see now is love around me

176

Where is there to Go …When it's up to Me

When everything seems so doomed
I let my imagination take over
Into a inner world where all is like heaven
I can create all I want
That seems to make me feel better
Like a higher plane, a higher vibe

Oh yes its all up to me
Oh so clearly I see
That when things bring me down
I just take my power back
And go into my mind
Where all is possible is what I find

It's my getaway, I just go zoom
Then I am in my mind imagining what I like
Then next thing I know
My reality starts to follow
That's creating reality
Our natural instinct, the nature of it all

So next time your down and out
Take some great advice
Don't stay in that low mood
Go inside inward into your mind
Let your imagination go
Imagine your greatest desires,
then you'll know for yourself

AnnaMarie Antoski

THE CITY OF FUN

It's always fun in the city
Wherever I go there's someone to talk to
and get to know
So many friendly opportunities just waiting in line
To meet someone new
Or visit more shops, and stop for some lunch
Observing the traffic with people rushing to and fro
With busy days and busy nights
I just love to sit above the brow
And watch everything flow

Sirens, horns and people stopped at crosswalks
There's just so much going on
I Surrender to it all and sit mesmerized
Basking in all these delights
Soon I'll be back to the silent serenity of country home
The fun of the city will be a lingering echo sketched in my
memory
I love them both, city and country,
two different ways to experience, enjoy and explore

Come with me over the Rainbow

Do you want to ride the waves
Into a world where only magic resides
Showing us our real true source
That life is really filled with love
And everyday is filled with bliss
Everything we imagine just becomes real

Come with me over the rainbow
Where life is so free
All doubt and troubles have melted
And there are only all possibilities

Most days I wished so passionately
That I would find real peace
Where all my wished did come true
That I was a god creating too

Where I could fly just like the birds
And sit upon the puffy skies

Some will say get back to reality
But I do it all the time
That's the power of thy mind

The old world sits in much disbelief
This is the new world that is becoming so free
And it takes the greatest power
To achieve those kinds of results
Which is to use the power of imagining
Held on long enough then you will see
Just like me
It does become physical

AnnaMarie Antoski

How we Swing our Magic Wand

When I feel like a victim
I ventured farther into the unknown
To know how to break the chains
So victimhood can no longer reign
Into the deep inner self
That the real source removes of pain

To my everlasting joy
There is a place to come alive
And know that we are the creators
Creating everything we experience
It becomes what we believe it to be
Just the way you think to expect
Is just exactly what you get

It's like being a magical wand
The only thing is most don't know what's really going on
Until you go into the unknown to know
You will get all the proof it will show
Your thoughts are the wand
Creating with every focus you give it

Good or bad just doesn't matter
Just like poof it will be created
So you can learn through all the contrast
Of what you truly do really want
Think it, focus. feel it
You're doing it all the time
Piercing the unknown it just becoming to know

TAKE YOUR POWER BACK

Have you had enough just like me
Thinking we had some integrity
When truly enslaved playing the conformed game
Till all our power is sucked away
Leaving with only drudgery, that's how fear plays the game
No more running, no more doubt
Threatening till I pout
When it was the enslavement that kept me rung
I no longer want to play this game that's perpetually spun

All the hype the media conditions to forsake
Create scenarios running rampant in our heads
When we could be instead be focusing on visions
That we desire instead of all this dread

All the things I bought into that I know now are not true
I am reformed and won't do what you want me to
I will live in the present in empowerment
Left to create of what I only want

Let the power go back to the people
The ninety percent who have carried the cross
The ones who can surely create the embittered world
Where wealth is shared not hoarded for just a few

Just Around the Corner

Do you believe in the all possible
Or you just feeling too hopeless to discover
That no matter what you are going through
There is a genie awaiting in you

Just around the corner is a miracle about to happen
Just around the corner something magical is to be
Just around the corner is all possibilities
All it takes it just one wish, just some thoughts, just some
feelings
To create all that you want to be

Do you still believed you are doomed
Then you're ready for a new vibe
One that will take you to new visions
The one's you've been dreaming of all your life

There's always down and there's always up
Deep in despair is the key to the magic
Once it's released it becomes back to chaos
The openness is ready to fill it up with miracles

ALL THE MAGIC IS INSIDE YOU

It's a better world you will find
Once the ego is merged with the soul
And spirit of no time
Love will reign, you'll feel high
And all power will be neutralized
When we follow our own hearts of our true selves
Magic will surely come back, released of all doubt

How to feel up when you feel so down
How to keep faith when there's none to be found
How to believe when life's been so hard
How to create when all externally is just hell

Take your power back
To let love shower on you
You focus inside
To where the real you is hidden
Find that peace
Holding on to it will let it all flow out
All the magic's inside of you

AnnaMarie Antoski

Just Letting it Flow

Missing the blossoming of another brand new day
  Of new inspirations, new ideas to come my way

The field of ecstasy as bliss fills the air
  Again to experience the magnificence of technology
    Within a whimsical second that our thoughts
      which instantaneously converts from our inner minds
        to the finger tips unto the keyboard
          Then transfers onto a screen page
            and as soon as we click
              the send button it appears so many miles
                away onto your screen to be received

To just stop and think about the awesomeness of how it works
  Brings much gratitude for our lives
              in how easily and magnificently
        It's when we take it all for granted that we miss
                    the divine beauty of it all

Genuine
Unconditional
Love

Unconditional love,
surely comes from the heart
Not a day ever goes by
that you judge, pout or sigh

You always share the best of you
Overfilled with excitement
that's continually renewed
Emotions you sure do express
Role modeling your very best
Of every moment being present
Of your never ending
unconditional love
that's always from your heart

AnnaMarie Antoski

Chapter 9

Fun

and

Joy

with

Deeper Wonderings

AnnaMarie Antoski

STRESS to *Bliss*

It's so easy to fall into stress
If we react to those old beliefs again
So many times it goes unnoticed
And before we know it we've repeated the old programs

It does take practice, I am sure by now you know
When it's done enough times
You'll start to feel the glow
Of problem that used to stress you out
Won't trigger you as much
Because you've created a better memory
To retrieve to respond without a doubt

We can take any stress and transform it into bliss
But we can also take and strip our bliss back to stress
What's it worth when it only breaks down our immune system
Yet it's addictive just like prescriptions

What's the key to making the shift
Creating new memories in association with bliss
By responding differently then in the past
Doing that over and over again
Changes everything, you'll see the proof for yourself
Just as long as you hang in long enough
And not let old reactions get in the way

Fun with Clouds

Such a relaxing color blue
The color of our throat area, the 5th charka of
Sky blue
With puffy white clouds reminds me of cotton balls
So soft and fuzzy when we imagine touching them
With our imagination when we let it run free
Unobstructed with possibilities
But they move by so quickly until I hold it in my focus
Then for a few moments I can create them to be what I want
Swirling into any becoming
Like this big teddy bear with a long tale
And just a little hole for its mouth
Enough to allow it to say hello

DEEPER INTO THE WEATHER

The sunny day turns so dark
As the clouds form above
Yet above all the clouds
The sun's still shining so bright
Down here for us in this town
The storm is rumbling its fierce sound

The rain becomes intense
Pouring down soaking everything in its path
As I look to the west
The sky still is so bright
I call a friend just to see
If it's stormy where they live

No she says, not even a drop
The sun is shining oh so bright

I love these subtle hints
That reveal secrets of reality and how it just may work
Of jet streams in the air
All depending on the way the wind blows
Yet deeper inside is more mysteries that lurk
If you're brave enough to explore the workings inside

Deep wondering what creates the atmosphere
And the wind that shows itself as it blows

Motion pushing through its flair
Stirring all the atoms they tow
That is invisible to our perception
If we have not expanded our conception
Of all that seems invisible yet is continuous movement
So we can eavesdrop to be revealed

Illusions make it appear like we're separate
As if we are not apart of the air
Yet the deeper we go
Like a microscope of consciousness
We will find all united, connected to it all
As we peak at our emotions
And how they do form in the atmosphere

We choose and think thoughts
Mostly so unconsciously without further to be sought
Yet those thoughts we are thinking
Are not dead ended structures
They are energy just like what you and me
And everything we experience to perceive
Is all energy that only illusions create an escape
To know what's revealing to show of its fate

Thoughts build into e-motion
Fueled with a strong potion
That gathers its momentum and becomes what we feel
If we ponder even further
Where do all these emotional feelings go
We will find invisibly they are connected
To everything including the air molecules
That is intertwined in the jet stream
Of the invisible air surrounding us all

Just as everyone and everything
Eventually has expression to release

Is the same way with our emotions
Like a boiling pot with its tightened lid
When it reaches it's boiling high state
It will overflow blowing off its tight lid
Overflowing, we see the results

Our emotions are the same
We let them out in invisible release
You could perceive it as a human volcano
Irrupting all the time
Emotions gathered and fueled
Expressed in so many ways that go so unnoticed
Overflowing into the atmosphere of invisible atoms of molecules
Fueled and explode as rain, snow, ice, storms, earthquakes,
Hurricanes, tornado's what we label and call weather
See the we in the word, we-ather will give us the clue

Its pure pettiness when most dismiss
That we are connected to everyone and everything
Affecting all we perceive
Just by our thoughts of energy
So energetically connected
In the future of our evolution
These truths will be revealed and accepted
The biggest crime then should be
If we don't take this unified field seriously
To be responsible for our thoughts
Because they are holistically creating everything
We will no longer be deceived

How prehistoric can we be
When we refuse to allow ourselves to believe to see
That we are connected so energetically
To everything through thoughts and emotions
One day all will see and believe

AnnaMarie Antoski

DARK
MATTER

It's been known for oh so long
From peering into our universe they've found
Dark matter is over three quarters more
 of the visible space of what we see as its core

What is dark matter that has all in the scientific minds so focused
To find out why we have more dark matter
 then anything else in our universal world
As they try to make the unknown known
So that they can understand our reality that's still unbeknown

Venturing farther and farther out they do go
When all the deepest of seeming mysterious secrets
 are in our own self to know
Though it does take an open mind
To look so deep into ourselves so we can find
That we are the secret waiting to reveal
All that we do but never realize to see
That it will always start with thee
As we go inside ourselves
Into the dark matter void we'll find
Infinite dimensions unfolded in and out of our linear time
The visible of matter is the invisible other side
One day we will see as the veils become thinner
All spiritual invisibility we no longer have to hide

Let Passion Become Your Life

I though I knew what passion was
But just like all knowledge is never really known
Until we feel it to experience it
Is when we become the wisdom of it
For the real truth to be dawned

Passion is experiencing every day life to be free
That days are no longer structured by the clock
Passion transforms every single task
Into a blossoming of love at last

Relaxed and free for extended hours
Doing something that you love that never sours
So immersed the hours goes by so fast
That when you look at the clock so much time has passed
How passion sustained such infinity to sew
Those ten hours went by like less then a minute
Then you know you were in passions eternal flow

Everything flows so joyfully
Nothing alters you to experience the passing of time
Ions become swirled into all you experience
You feel as if you really are in another world of a different kind

AnnaMarie Antoski

Unidentified Flying Object

All is so quiet, all is so dark
Just the bright lit sky showing its sparking through space in time
Staring in wonder up above
Of what is suppose to be a past of explosive stars
Planets that seem of no existence but we hope to find
Living creatures that may be similar to us earthlings kind of mind

Then just out of the blue is a prickling of light
Not fading just becoming brighter
As it moves along the darkness of its corridors unconfined
Illuminating jet streams of many colors come brighter in my sight

Passing through our space in time
What are these alien of beings wanting to find
Maybe they are as curious as us
Yet they have advanced centuries ahead with exuberant thrust

The stream of colored lights glowing even brighter
As to my perception seems to be coming closer
I try to block my conditioned fears out
That they may be mean and kidnap me to dissect
I remind myself that's just an old memory fear
It's all law of attraction so I think love thoughts instead
Still it's coming closer and seems larger then ever
Of course my rational mind keeps wondering
Is it a jet or something I can interpret

Hovering it does for what seems like an eternity
As I kept my vision of perception trance in my focus
Then in an instant it just disappears
Or is it my perception that is no longer clear

What I See in Another

In the other I do see all that reflects back to me
I see love so very deep but not quite yet pure divinity
As there are still conditions to love I find
To love with no expectations and to just allow
Yet I still see so much fear and negativity
Still so much to work on to be eternally free
Though through all that I do see
Love that does extend in all sincerity

So easy it can be to blame
Again its cloaked in judgments game
In the past it would take awhile to catch myself
But now I notice it like a flick of a switch
To release the judgment that once used to persist
Knowing its me who's doing the perceiving
Quickly brings me back on the feel good track

Now what I see in another is my invisible radar
Transforming it to knowing its my indicator
Guiding me back on my loving path
As judgments only create more pain to sustain
To no longer relive the same lessons again
I found such comfort in reflections to be my friend
Through it all fragmented pieces I do mend

AnnaMarie Antoski

Love Potion Divine

*A most eternal love energized and sustains us all
So powerful It creates everything we know
All it takes is to channel into it for a bit to see
That it makes all and everything appear so loving
Irrelevant of what the camouflages shows
It is Seeded in everyone of us to know*

*Divine in every way, no polarity of negative or positive
Its all for the experience to continue to evolve
To perceive all and everything to be
Is to know our heritage and be one with it all in thee*

*Love potion divine intertwined from the infinite source
Most powerful and its in us all
As it become activated and grows as it flourishes
It radiates an aura of innocence
Love potion divine radiates
It happens when you become love*

*It's the creator of all that is
The blooming love we become
The seventh seal will open completely
And all magnificence will be our reflections
Enchanting the stirring in others
As they know it and feel it from their hearts*

The Secret of Falling out of Love

When we fall in love, we fall from grace
We feel up lifted, in a blissful ecstasy state
No matter what the other does
Its cute and exhilarating, they could do no wrong
Till the illusion of falling in love
Triggers a different kind of love song

As time passes, reality sets back in
Then comes the not liking part that just seems to begin
Many wonder how it can be
What changed that created the opposite state
When something was so cute becomes bothersome instead

When we fall in love, we fall from grace
Into personality fractured through duality's prismy shades
Giving quite the illusion that all is so perfect
Because falling in love, is really falling from grace

Yet its when we fall out of love
That's when real grace shows its face
When we love unconditionally
Its like taking off the illusionary shades
of what tripped us up
All part of the process to return to grace
Not to look for another to take the others place
We will only be generating the same fall again
There seems to be only one way out
And that's to be graceful love through it all

We know we're in grace again
When the other makes us feel so good
Then the other irritates and bothers us
But this time its understood
We love unconditionally
With allowing acceptance removed of judgments
Seeing the other through our own reflection
Is returning to loving grace
As judgments shows no more trace

Each time we transform a negative to a positive
We have the urge that will again transform
that positive into a negative
It's the swinging vibration of duality's game
Once played in it enough
We see the light and our real journey begins

We perpetually transform until we sit in graces paradox
Then we no longer perceive in the swinging back and forth
Instead experience everything and one as a part of the whole
Holographic becomes our nature
Then the falling in love of duplicity is known
And a realized process that was only the roadway to
Unconditional graceful love is what becomes known

We know full grace
When we welcome all falling in love's challenges
Transform it quick
To get back into graceful bliss
When what we see in any other
Is genuinely unconditional in every sense
Then we no longer fall in love
We continue to expand
In graces love
The highest vibration to be in

Enlightenment of Being in the Paradox

Swinging back and forth can be such fun in our lives
Till we know that it's a game we came to experience
Until all the contrast finally subsides
So that we can know great wisdom to own
Bringing all parts back to its original whole

It's a teetering tottering kind of ride
One day we're down and another day we're up
Filtering of negative and positive sides
Till all becomes being up, it's an up kind of jive

Making light of any darkness
Shining bright through every defined adversity
Finding the love seed in every single one and thing
Even if its seems so buried beneath

Everyone of us has an enlightenment seed
Will shine so bright once we are no longer deceived
Of the camouflages of good or bad, like or dislike of fear versus love
To feel and shine our light on all that once seemed dark

Being in the paradox is seeing both side
No more swinging of the pendulum of light or dark
Enlightenment blooms and shine so bright
We become to never alter from this genuine love state
As the dark parts of our soul become less of our fate

AnnaMarie Antoski

Breezy Fields of Wheat

So warm the heat of the summer breeze on my skin
As I allow my vision to permeate the hundreds of acres of field
covered in wheat
As the hot wind picks up as it brushed against the millions of stalks
Like golden strands the wheat looks like it's dancing
to the rhythm of nature and all that it flocks

I see in the far distance the deer's grazing in the wheat field
Two adult deer's and three younger ones
It must be a family
How playfully the youngin's romp about
while the sunsets its purity in the sky

Hundreds of acres of wheat perpetually blowing in the wind
Appears to glisten seeming orchestrated by the summer breeze
Each stalk yet separate appears connected
Infinitely moving touching one another
Spreading its seeds through the moving wind
Taking it close or maybe far away it seems
Quite the focus it does take indeed
To just stay present to follow the summer breezy fields of wheat

BIG OLD LOVING TREE

As I sit under you and open myself up
So many stories you can tell me
Of decades upon decades that you have experienced
Not only the changing weather
That has strengthened you to the greatness you are today
But also of all the birds, insects and people
That you have experienced through all the decades

Tell me your stories, I so want to know
Of all the people that have shared time with you,
Just as I am right now
Tell me about all the insects, birds and animals
that you have shared your limbs with
for shade and security and even the woodpecker
that keeps picking at your bark,
oh how you show us such kind sharing unconditional love

I realize this is only a small part of you that we do see
Under the ground you stretch your roots
Almost so eternal and infinitely
Nourishing yourself to keep you strong
While sharing with everyone and thing that's all around

How your limbs and leaves dance with invigorating rhythm
in the wind
I thank you for all you have shown me
of nature and life
Such an endless exuberance you exude
How could anyone believe that you are just a tree
When there is so much more to you
That any of us could ever know to perceive

AnnaMarie Antoski

Little Toad
what
Reflection Do I See

Little toad, you just hopped over to me
  How you are so a part of thee
    Staring at me with your penetrating eyes
      maybe you are letting me know that I am on your turf
        though to me we're just sharing this space we both call earth

Continue to sit basking in the hot sun
  still staring at me I try to pick up
    of telepathy that might be going on
      all I pick up is you just want to be left alone
        so that you can catch some breakfast
          of the insects that are flying around

Jovially you squint your eyes
  then a giant hop to the insect you found
    back in place you sit and wait
      for the next bug that becomes your meal of your fate

How life feeds on life
  we see it all around
    Maybe one day we will evolve to find
      that we will be nourished just from the sun
        energetically charged and no longer have the instinct to eat
No more life feeding off life

instead we will be and feel complete

We are a Part of Thee

You hold this book within your hands
Though we seem like strangers, really its illusionary
We like everything else is spiritual energy
Though we seem so physical bound
That too is another illusion we can become to see through I found

As I write in my present
You are reading in my future
But if I remote view into the future
Like right now as I stop to focus
I can feel your presence already lingering
Removed from times continuity
Unbounded from man made time in space
Being in the state of being simultaneous
Is the freedom to travel to all spiritual territory

So as you read and hold this book
I in my future do behold
The energy that lingers upon each page of written word
Of a being that is connected unveiled of illusions
No longer fooled of believing
Knowing we are more then our physical body and ego
We are connected in the unified sense
Picking up on so much more when we just let go
By focusing on what we want to know
That you are here and I am here
Sharing the same page of energy
Removed from time and experiencing infinite space
I experience you of a being of grace

AnnaMarie Antoski

Also by AnnaMarie Antoski

Infinite Manifesting

The Hidden Key Orgasm Reveals

Evolving Reality of Bewitched

Stumbling Through Infinity
Heart Reflection Poetry

Knowledge Transforms to Wisdom
Expanding Consciousness Poetry

ABOUT THE AUTHOR

AnnaMarie Antoski has studied the nature of reality for over two decades with consistent passion and integrated what she has learned into her life experiences. Sharing her self healing and evolving psychic abilities she has become an inspiration in her field of experiences.

Website: http://www.infinite-manifesting.org/

May You Forever
Enjoy!
G.G.

Made in the USA
Charleston, SC
23 June 2011